Simula SpringerBriefs on Computing

Volume 8

Springer and Simula have launched a new book series, *Simula SpringerBriefs on Computing*, which aims to provide introductions to select research in computing. The series presents both a state-of-the-art disciplinary overview and raises essential critical questions in the field. Published by SpringerOpen, all *Simula SpringerBriefs on Computing* are open access, allowing for faster sharing and wider dissemination of knowledge.

Simula Research Laboratory is a leading Norwegian research organization which specializes in computing. The book series will provide introductory volumes on the main topics within Simula's expertise, including communications technology, software engineering and scientific computing.

By publishing the *Simula SpringerBriefs on Computing,* Simula Research Laboratory acts on its mandate of emphasizing research education. Books in this series are published only by invitation from a member of the editorial board.

More information about this series at http://www.springer.com/series/13548

Jo Erskine Hannay

Benefit/Cost-Driven Agile Software Development

with Benefit Points and Size Points

Jo Erskine Hannay
Center for Effective Digitalization
of the Public Sector (EDOS)
Simula Metropolitan
Center for Digital Engineering
Oslo, Norway

ISSN 2512-1677   ISSN 2512-1685   (electronic)
Simula SpringerBriefs on Computing
ISBN 978-3-030-74217-1   ISBN 978-3-030-74218-8   (eBook)
https://doi.org/10.1007/978-3-030-74218-8

Mathematics Subject Classification: 91-XX, 94-XX

This Springer imprint is published by the registered company Springer Nature Switzerland AG
The registered company address is: Gewerbestrasse 11, 6330 Cham, Switzerland

Foreword

Dear reader,

Our aim with the series *Simula SpringerBriefs on Computing* is to provide compact introductions to selected fields of computing. Entering a new field of research can be quite demanding for graduate students, postdocs, and experienced researchers alike: the process often involves reading hundreds of papers, and the methods, results and notation styles used often vary considerably, which makes for a time-consuming and potentially frustrating experience. The briefs in this series are meant to ease the process by introducing and explaining important concepts and theories in a relatively narrow field, and by posing critical questions on the fundamentals of that field. A typical brief in this series should be around 100 pages and should be well suited as material for a research seminar in a well-defined and limited area of computing.

We have decided to publish all items in this series under the SpringerOpen framework, as this will allow authors to use the series to publish an initial version of their manuscript that could subsequently evolve into a full-scale book on a broader theme. Since the briefs are freely available online, the authors will not receive any direct income from the sales; however, remuneration is provided for every completed manuscript. Briefs are written on the basis of an invitation from a member of the editorial board. Suggestions for possible topics are most welcome and can be sent to aslak@simula.no.

January 2016

Prof. Aslak Tveito
CEO

Dr. Martin Peters
Executive Editor Mathematics
Springer Heidelberg, Germany

Preface

To produce value – or benefit – for stakeholders has always been the reason for initiating information technology (IT) development projects. In our work as researchers and consultants in IT project management, we are witnessing an increasing focus on benefits, and there is a great deal of talk on benefits management in IT project management communities. National and international bodies (NATO being one of the largest) now include benefits management, in some form, more explicitly in their IT strategies.

This could be because there have been several recent incidents where projects and programmes have not been delivering the intended value. This is, of course, nothing new. Moreover – and although benefits management is almost as old as project management itself – there seems to be bewilderment regarding how to perform this 'management of benefits'. We observe that, despite the rather obvious importance of delivering benefit, businesses often resort to managing their portfolios and projects according to what amounts to a heavy emphasis on cost control only.

Our impression is that it is possible to talk about benefits management and even to make sensible diagrams outlining the main phases in benefits management, but that it is hard to actually perform benefits management. Project workers do not know what to do when it comes to benefits management in their daily project work.

Benefits management, as outlined by many authors over the past years, involves a number of phases throughout the IT development and production life cycle. This book introduces and elaborates on one single technique: that of assigning benefit estimates in the form of benefit points to product elements. This technique is inherently bound to the development phase, but we will argue that, if one does assign benefit estimates this way, one will be better equipped to perform other benefits management activities elsewhere in the life cycle.

Just as story points for estimating cost do not solve the entire problem of cost management, benefit points *a fortiori* do not solve the entire problem of benefits management. Benefits management involves organizational, socio-behavioural, and political issues that are addressed by their own disciplines in academia and practice. However, just as numerical cost estimates provide a tool for managing costs, benefit points provide a tool for benefits management.

This book presents a few *base techniques* for using benefit points in combination with story points (or size points as we will call them). These techniques are tools for managing projects with a focus on both cost and benefit. They are base techniques because they provide methodological skeletons that must be instantiated and adapted to the particular situation. We style the techniques in the terminology of agile management and development, but of the ideas can be used in other and related process models as well, such as DevOps, BizDev, etc. Agile, in our context, is the present-day notion that includes planning and monitoring, in other words, what we consider systematizing agile principles. This is especially relevant for larger projects with several teams.

We provide examples from private and public sector organizations that have used one or several of the base techniques. As of this writing, no single organization has implemented all the base techniques. It is our hope that this text will help organizations adopt and adapt these techniques to their projects and portfolio management processes. The use of benefit points will make it possible to generate empirical evidence on the effects of benefits management.

This text is intended for private and public sector IT professionals familiar with agile development and management. The text acknowledges project and portfolio management as a discipline proper, for which you should have an explicit and conscious attitude to methodology. This text might therefore challenge you, rather than simply make you feel good by confirming things you already know or follow. Project and portfolio management is not for the faint-hearted, and too many projects attract unfortunate attention due to bad leadership. Taking the job seriously means investing well-spent effort to become stronger. We think that mastering any of the techniques in this book will make you better equipped for the job.

The core ideas in this book were initially developed for a course in agile project management providing Project Management Professional (PMP) certification (Project Management Institute). The ideas were further developed in *IEEE Software* articles.[1,2,3] The material has been substantially reworked for this book. A running example appears throughout the text that. It is a simplistic artificial example designed to illustrate the techniques.

How to read this book: Some sections are optional and can be safely skipped in the first reading. These sections are marked by an asterisk (*). They include advanced topics with technical elaborations, as well as background information, ideas for further use of the techniques in this book, and topics that address interesting questions that practitioners have asked us.

Oslo, March 2020   *Jo Erskine Hannay*

---

[1] J. E. Hannay, H. C. Benestad & K. Strand (2017): Benefit Points: The Best Part of the Story, *IEEE Software* 34(3), 73–85.

[2] J. E. Hannay, H. C. Benestad & K. Strand (2017): Earned Business Value: See That You Deliver Value to Your Customer, *IEEE Software* 34(4), 58–70.

[3] J. E. Hannay, H. C. Benestad & K. Strand (2019): Agile Uncertainty Assessment for Benefit Points and Story Points, *IEEE Software* 36(4), 50–62.

Acknowledgements

This text would not have been possible without the extensive project leader experience of Kjetil Strand and Hans Christian Benestad. They were both instrumental in developing the methods in this book and co-authored the initial articles in *IEEE Software*, but too busy running projects and putting our ideas into action to spend time writing this book. This book would also not have been possible without the support of Magne Jørgensen at the *Centre for Effective Digitalization of the Public Sector* (EDOS). Jørgensen's extensive past and present empirical research on estimation and benefits management forms the motivational backdrop for the techniques presented in this book.

We are grateful for the valuable feedback, comments, and insights of our collaborators at PROMIS AS, Verdix AS, and Metier Academy AS; the participants in the IT Project Professional certification programme; and other practitioners who have applied the methods in this book. We are also grateful for the development and modernization projects in which we have worked and conducted studies. These activities directly inspired the techniques presented in this book.

Contents

Chapter 1
Business Value Disadvantaged

> What the customer buys and considers value is never a product. It is always utility, that is, what a product or a service does for the customer.
>
> PETER DRUCKER

Abstract Despite the current emphasis on benefit in stakeholders' minds, there is still a focus on cost management when it comes down to the day-to-day work in modern software development. This works counter to underlying assumptions in modern development methodology. We motivate a more deliberate approach to benefits management during development, but it is the *combination* of cost and benefits management that saves the day.

1.1 A Paradoxical Emphasis on Cost

Modern development ideals focus on business value. In agile management and development, the mantra is 'Value for the customer'. The product owner is involved along the way and backlogs are prioritized, with the best intent to produce benefit. Yet, it seems that, in many information technology development projects, there is still bewilderment regarding how exactly customer value should be expressed in process decisions.

Routines for cost estimation are common, and cost estimates and productivity outlooks are routinely updated and monitored. Earned value measures and burndown charts can tell you when to start cutting back the scope. However, chances are that benefit is treated haphazardly compared to cost [5], which is a paradox, given the focus that business value is supposed to have.

This book promotes the idea that one should treat benefit with at least the same systematic attention as one treats cost. Moreover, benefit and cost estimates should be combined to give estimates of benefit over cost in a manner that enables *benefit/cost-driven development*.

The absence of an explicit treatment of benefit can lead to decisions based only on cost when one actually wishes to make decisions based on business value. It would be good if one could use a burndown chart to cut or promote functionality on the grounds of benefit rather than cost only.

© The Author(s) 2021
J. E. Hannay, *Benefit/Cost-Driven Agile Software Development*,
Simula SpringerBriefs on Computing 8,
https://doi.org/10.1007/978-3-030-74218-8_1

Further, one is in danger of perceiving an expensive piece of functionality as also representing a lot of benefit. This fallacy piggybacks on the folkloristic *common law of business balance* [13], that is, the principle that one cannot pay a little and receive a lot: one should have to pay more for more of a product (ten bottles of wine) than for less of that product (two bottles of the same wine). The principle applies to software development as well; it is reasonable to expect to pay more for more software than for less software.

However, more software does not necessarily provide functionality that delivers more benefit. The confounding of cost with benefit transforms the reasonable principle above into a fallacy.

Clearly, then, there is another dimension to take heed of, in addition to the *amount of software* or even the *amount of functionality*. Thus, unless one has a sensible measure of benefit for one's backlog, one will not be able to manage construction with respect to benefit and will potentially regress to merely producing amounts of software instead.

1.2   Taking Control ...

Management based explicitly on benefit, in addition to cost, implies steering development activities toward the intended goal. It should also help you to avoid phenomena such as the *escalation of commitment to a failing course of action* in general [15, 16], and in software development in particular [7, 8]. This phenomenon involves people continuing to pursue activities in the face of clear signs that the activities are not achieving the goals, due to an (often emotional) attachment to the effort already invested in the activities. Related to this are the *sunk cost effect* and the *Concorde effect*, wherein a rationale is created to continue an ostensibly failing course of action, with the argument of not wasting what has already been invested [1].

A business strategy with plans that express development metrics explicitly in terms of business value and cost is a valuable tool to counter such effects. Suppose the strategy states that development will cease as soon as potential business value is no longer produced. Suppose, also, that metrics are in place that keep track of not only the amount of software produced (and money spent), but also the amount of benefit that the software is expected to give. Then, it should be impossible to enter into the realm of wilfully producing waste without at least someone in the steering group noticing.

1.3   ... with Agile

Agile promotes the frequent deployment of functionality. When agility is combined with wise architectural design in the form of parts of functionality that provide integral benefit (product elements), stopping development should be much less scary.

One should cease development when the benefit to cost can no longer be defended. If backlogs are ordered so that elements with high benefit over cost are realized first, then, by design, what has been produced and deployed until then already holds benefit. It is not so that everything goes to waste by stopping, so there is much less vulnerability to the sunk cost effect. In fact, what is then happening is not the *premature* cessation of development, but the *cessation of development just in time*.

Case 1. In 2013, a public sector welfare administration terminated its information technology modernization programme prematurely after about one and a half years' development. The total budget was about EUR 400 million at the time of writing, to be spent over six years. The sunk cost at termination was about EUR 180 million, of which EUR 36 million was spent on functionality that was never to be used [10, 11]. Generally presented in the press as yet another information technology scandal, the termination of the programme before all was lost was also applauded as a remarkably mature decision [19]. When things began to downhill, programme management took the courageous decision to stop before further losses, thus countering the sunk cost effect.

The ensuing revision pointed to several causes of failure. For example, the programme did not employ the idea of delivering integral functionality in manageable increments. Rather, it defined a total of only three excessively large projects and started with the largest and most complex of them. We also know that programme management did not find it worthwhile to update its skills on benefits management in the inception phase. The decision to halt the programme was made on the grounds of loss of control of costs, functionality, and architecture, rather than on explicit arguments of failure to deliver value for all that money.

Although the programme in the case above was halted before all was lost, this book offers techniques to help management stop even earlier, to save those EUR 36 million and even the EUR 180 million.

Benefits management [18] concerns an information system's entire life cycle. Since benefit is realized by using the system, benefits management concerns not just the system itself, but also how it is adopted and used in organizational and societal life.

Our focus is on techniques of benefits management that are performed during the development phases. We define our techniques in terms of incremental development, which involves stakeholders using – and obtaining benefit from – early deployed functionality. This means that the techniques do concern using the system, beyond developing it. The techniques are, however, for estimating and monitoring the system's expected benefit during these increments, and do not address organizational concerns as such.

Benefits management can be carried out in any software development model, including waterfall-based models. However, empirical results suggest that benefits management works better in a context with a flexible delivery scope, frequent deliveries, and extensive collection and use of feedback (see [5, 6] for pointers).

1.4 Benefit/Cost-Driven Development Methodology

A recent study [5] has found that projects that perceived themselves as successful in delivering the expected benefits differed from less successful ones, in that

- they applied benefits management practices before and during project execution,
- they applied core agile practices of frequent delivery to the client and scope flexibility,
- their clients were deeply involved in these practices.

This corroborates evidence from other empirical studies, suggesting that companies that engage in benefits management perform better in terms of most success criteria, especially those related to better project control and greater success in realized benefits [3, 6, 9, 12, 17]. Better project control, here, relates to updated information on projects' status and productivity.

However, benefits management has not achieved satisfactory uptake. In the words of Brees, Jenner, Serra, and Thorpe [2],

> It is now about 25 years since the emergence of benefits management, but hitherto it has had limited impact on project management and even less on general management practices. This is despite evidence that a focus on benefits improves the success rate of projects and programmes.

Respondents to Jørgensen's study [5] reported a lack of methodological support for benefits management. In particular, they experienced a lack of support in *quantifying the relation between planned returns and product elements*.

This book has been written to help you with that. However, just as management by cost alone is not enough, it would not be sensible to go to the other extreme and manage by benefit alone. The message in this book is, therefore, to combine cost management and benefits management.

In the following chapters, we will present techniques for estimating the benefit of the system under development and how that can be combined with cost estimates. We address a small but vital part of benefits management and provide numerical tools for use in various phases of benefits management.

1.5 Design

The development of our techniques follows the steps of design science [4]: design an artefact according to design principles, deploy the artefact to the field, learn from observations, and redesign. Here, the artefact is the techniques that we develop, and the design principles involve the following.

Concreteness: The techniques should be designed for performing concrete tasks. There can be many reasons why benefit estimation is not common; a lack of concrete techniques will leave project stakeholders and workers in the dark as to what to do, even if they grasp the general idea of benefits management.

Noninvasiveness: The techniques should be designed to be used in the existing process flow. If methods are too complex or too invasive in day-to-day work, they will not be employed. New techniques are often perceived as invasive, regardless.

Satisficing: The techniques should be designed to be *good enough* for the tasks at hand and in line with what Herbert Simon [14] calls *satisficing*, rather than optimizing. This point is essential for the simple and time-efficient use of techniques.

Support for cognitive processes: The techniques should be designed based on research in the field of judgement and decision making, to suit the nature of the cognitive processes involved in assessment.

Recognizability: The techniques should be reminiscent of existing techniques of state of practice to facilitate adoption.

Since there is a current lack of methodology, or at least a lack of reported use of any methodology, for conducting benefits management at the level and form presented in this book, there is no empirical evidence (systematic observations or analysis) to suggest precisely how effective our ideas are. Therefore, it is essential that projects start to use techniques so that the effects of benefits management can be evaluated. This book contributes such techniques. In due course, then, field studies can be conducted to evaluate the use of these techniques.

References

1. H.R. Arkes and P. Ayton, "The Sunk Cost and Concorde Effects: Are humans less rational than lower animals?" *Psychological Bulletin*, vol. 25, no. 5, pp. 591–600, 1999.
2. R. Breese, S. Jenner, C.E.M. Serra, and J. Thorp, "Benefits management: Lost or found in translation," *International Journal of Project Management*, vol. 33, no. 7, pp. 1438–1451, 2015.
3. A. Budzier and B. Flyvbjerg, "Making sense of the impact and importance of outliers in project management through the use of power laws," in *Proc. International Research Network on Organizing by Projects (IRNOP)*, vol. 11, 2013, pp. 228–232.
4. A.R. Hevner, S.T. March, and J. Park, "Design science in information systems research," *MIS Quarterly*, pp. 76–106, Mar. 2004.
5. M. Jørgensen, "A survey of the characteristics of projects with success in delivering client benefits," *Information and Software Technology*, vol. 78, pp. 83–94, 2016.
6. M. Jørgensen, P. Mohagheghi, and S. Grimstad, "Direct and indirect connections between type of contract and software project outcome," *International J. Project Management*, vol. 35, no. 8, pp. 1573–1586, 2017.
7. M. Keil, J. Mann, and A. Rai, "Why software projects escalate: An empirical analysis and test of four theoretical models," *MIS Quarterly*, vol. 24, no. 4, pp. 631–664, 2000.
8. M. Keil, A. Rai, J. Mann, and G. Zhang, "Why software projects escalate: The importance of project management constructs," *IEEE Transactions on Engineering Management*, vol. 50, no. 3, pp. 251–261, 2003.

9. C. Lin and Y.C. Liu, "Evaluation issues in managing IS/IT outsourcing contracts: A study of large Australian organizations." in *Collaborative Decision Making in the Internet Era*, 2005.
10. J. Lystad, "Det er ingen skam å snu – erfaringer fra Mattilsynet og NAV," Presentation given at Conf. of the Agency for Public Management and eGovernment (Difi), Dec. 6, 2017.
11. S. Olaussen, Ø. Tendal, S. Johansen, V. Sem, S. Bråthen, H. Bremnes, E. Grubbmo, and A.D. Ræder, "KSP-rapport nr. 1 for Modernisering av IKT i NAV – Rapport til Finansdepartementet og Arbeids- og sosialdepartementet, Versjon: 1.0," 2015.
12. C.E.M. Serra and M. Kunc, "Benefits realisation management and its influence on project success and on the execution of business strategies," *Interntional J. Project Management*, vol. 33, no. 1, pp. 53–66, 2015.
13. F.R. Shapiro, *The Yale Book of Quotations*.   Yale University Press, 2006.
14. H.A. Simon, *The Sciences of the Artificial*, 3rd ed.   MIT Press, 1996.
15. B.M. Staw, "Knee-deep in the big muddy: A study of escalating commitment to a chosen course of action," *Organizational Behavior and Human Performance*, vol. 16, no. 1, pp. 2–44, 1976.
16. B.M. Staw, "The escalation of commitment: An update and appraisal," in *Organizational Decision Making*, Z. Shapira, Ed.   Cambridge University Press, 1997, ch. 9, pp. 191–215.
17. A. ul Musawir, C.E.M. Serra, O. Zwikael, and I. Ali, "Project governance, benefit management, and project success: Towards a framework for supporting organizational strategy implementation," *International J. Project Management*, vol. 35, no. 8, pp. 1658–1672, 2017.
18. J. Ward and E. Daniel, *Benefits Management: How to Increase the Business Value of Your IT Projects. 2nd Edition.*   Wiley, 2012.
19. E. Zachariassen, "Nav stanser IT-prosjekt til 3,3 milliarder – Moderniseringsprogrammet var feil metode. Nav får skryt fra statlig ekspert," article published Oct. 25, 2013.

Chapter 2
Benefit Points – An Overview

> If you can't measure it, you can't improve it.
>
> PETER DRUCKER

Abstract We give a nontechnical overview of the main techniques in this book. It all starts with providing benefit estimates in the form of benefit points. Combining benefit estimates and cost estimates produces a benefit-cost index, with which one can order and reorder backlogs. Benefit points also offer a way to monitor and control the construction of beneficial functionality, not just the amount of functionality. Benefit points and size points can be instantiated with monetary values that reflect bad, most likely, and good case scenarios based on uncertainty assessments.

2.1 Benefit Estimates

Benefit/cost-driven development as presented in this book hinges on a very simple idea: you should provide benefit estimates in addition to cost estimates to your product elements (Fig. 2.1).

For now, think of a product element as an integral piece of functionality that provides value for business. In the context of incremental development, we will later be considering product elements in the form of minimum viable products (MVPs) [8]. MVPs are gradually maturing increments of functionality that can be deployed for the early assessment of both benefit and cost.[1] However, we will also see that it is possible to view entire projects as product elements.

This book is about assigning benefit estimates in the form of benefit points. The notion of benefit points is analogous to story points used for cost estimation. Both types of points are assigned to product elements. Numerical scales, such as the Fibonacci numbers or the numbers one to 100, are used to express relative contributions, rather than absolute estimates. Thus, relative benefit estimation involves comparing product elements with regards to benefit – how much benefit a product element represents compared to another; 18 versus five, say – without assigning abso-

---

[1] See, for example, https://www.linkedin.com/pulse/mvp-bike-car-fred-voorhorst for an intuition on MVPs.

© The Author(s) 2021
J. E. Hannay, *Benefit/Cost-Driven Agile Software Development*,
Simula SpringerBriefs on Computing 8,
https://doi.org/10.1007/978-3-030-74218-8_2

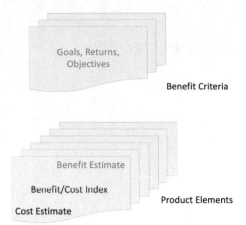

Goals, Returns,
Objectives

Benefit Criteria

Benefit Estimate

Benefit/Cost Index

Cost Estimate

Product Elements

Fig. 2.1 The basic mechanisms for benefit/cost-driven development: assign benefit estimates to product elements, in addition to cost estimates.

lute estimates in terms of benefit metrics. This approach reuses techniques familiar from cost estimation, such as group consensus-based wideband Delphi techniques [1] and planning poker for assigning story points [2]. We will describe techniques for assigning benefit points in Chapters 3 and 4.

With benefits as the *raison d'être* for development projects, we want to promote benefit points as expressing an essential part of the user story, to balance the one-sided emphasis on cost estimates for project control.

2.2 Benefit Criteria

Benefit estimation requires explicit criteria for assessing benefit. These criteria should be part of, or linked to, a project's business case, portfolio directives, the customer organization's strategic goals, and so forth (Fig. 2.1). Benefit can be expressed in terms of various metrics (person-hours, number of errors, efficiency metrics, etc.), depending on which criteria one is using. In this respect, benefit estimation is fundamentally different from cost estimation. This book will describe how one can combine benefit estimates on diverse criteria into a single benefit estimate for a product element.

2.3 Management by Benefit/Cost

With both benefit estimates and cost estimates, one can construct a benefit-cost index for the product elements (Fig. 2.1, in blue). This approach relies on being able

Fig. 2.2 Ordered backlog according to decreasing benefit/cost.

to express benefit in a single estimate, as mentioned above. The benefit-cost index allows one to prioritize which product elements to put into construction and decide when to stop construction in a particular backlog. Figure 2.2 illustrates the idea where a benefit-cost index that equals one indicates an equal benefit-to-cost ratio, so that anything smaller indicates a product element whose costs are estimated at more than its benefits.

Such an index provides explicit and consensual grounds for vital decisions. The intention is now to stop deliberately, just in time, and not too late, by mistake.

One can use the index to decide where in the queue a new proposed piece of functionality belongs, possibly bumping product elements with lower benefit/cost further down the queue (see Fig. 2.3). If there happens to be a time or cost limit and more of the backend of the backlog is pushed behind that limit, this will result in more functionality being dropped in favour of better functionality in benefit-cost terms.

Case 2. A public sector organization managing governmental investments, loans, and pensions was running a EUR 100 million development project to replace their pension management system. The project consisted of 10 Scrum teams that were coordinated by cross-cutting architecture and testing teams. In the final stages of the project, the product owner asked project management to incorporate seven new epics (product elements). While clearly a disruptive request at that late, hectic stage, the project manager remained calm and took time out to conduct a benefits assessment of the proposed epics and remaining backlog with the product owner and relevant stakeholders. The new epics were estimated to yield a high benefit, and, after a cost analysis, they were incorporated into the remaining backlog at the appropriate place. Some of the functionality in the backlog was also found to be better covered by the new epics. The seven new epics bumped existing epics with lower benefit/cost down the line. In the end, the tail end of the backlog was cancelled, with no regrets, saving the product owner approximately EUR 5 million.

The project in the case above did not systematically maintain benefit estimates for each product element in the backlog. Still, project management appreciated the benefits of benefits management and had sufficient clout in the organization to perform an ad hoc benefit-cost analysis at a crucial stage in the project. The techniques

Fig. 2.3 Ordered backlog with a new element bumping elements of lower benefit/cost back down the line.

in this book are meant to help projects maintain running benefit/cost estimates, so that stakeholders can make wise decisions, such as that illustrated in the case, as a matter of routine during development.

Projects can use the benefit-cost index to monitor, adjust, and report on construction progress, in terms of benefit, as well as cost. Following a tactic of constructing the product elements with the highest benefit/cost first, the plan will look like the solid blue line in Fig. 2.4, where a large proportion of the potential benefit is constructed relative to costs early and the accumulated benefit-cost ratio tapers off as less benefit/cost-productive product elements are encountered in the backlog.

Infrastructure and architectural product elements that do not produce immediate benefits for end users [3, 4] should also be included here. Benefit estimation involves estimating the benefit for all relevant stakeholders, including those responsible for further incremental development and maintenance. Architectural modernization can also yield benefit by enabling interoperability with other systems.

Case 3. A development team in a telecommunications company was struggling with a 20-year old legacy system that interacted with over 70 other systems. Although it was one of the company's most successful systems, the development team was experiencing increasing requests for changes and adaptations to meet market demands. A modernization project to refurbish the system was clearly overdue. However, the team faced the challenge of convincing portfolio management to initiate such a project. The team systematized their argument using architectural epics whose contributions to maintenance, integration, and further development efficiency metrics were assessed in a relative manner, using benefit points. Assigning monetary value to the benefit points, the teams argued that the modernization project would give the company a competitive edge in the long run. The project was initiated, and the team subsequently used their benefit estimates during the project to prioritize their epics.

A plan such as that represented by the solid blue line in Fig. 2.4 can be accompanied by bad-case (pessimistic) and good-case (optimistic) estimates, as illustrated by the dashed blue lines in Fig. 2.4. Such good- and bad-case estimates arise from uncertainty assessment, which we will cover in Chapter 6. When both benefit estimates and cost estimates are expressed in terms of relative points, one can instantiate the points with different monetary values that express the most likely scenario together with good- and bad-case scenarios, without redoing all the product element estimates.

The actual construction productivity can be plotted against this plan, as indicated by the orange line in Fig. 2.4. Note that one can now plot productivity against planned benefit, in addition to planned cost. This feature adds the benefit dimension to project progress reporting, in addition to the traditionally one-dimensional focus on cost productivity. We will elaborate on this point in Chapter 5.

2.4 Life Cycle Perspective

Note that the label on the orange line in Fig. 2.4 is 'adjusted' rather than 'actual'. Consider, for a moment, the traditional way of measuring productivity in terms of cost (or effort). Then, cost estimation concerns only the cost of development, and when product elements are constructed, one knows the actual cost. However, the addition of the benefit dimension requires an explicit *life cycle perspective*: the estimates of a product element's benefit pertain to what happens after that product element is deployed into production in the organization, after construction. So, to obtain a sensible expression of benefit/cost, estimates of cost must also consider the product element's life cycle, not only its construction. To emphasize this distinction, we will refer to the points used for cost estimation in our techniques as 'size points',

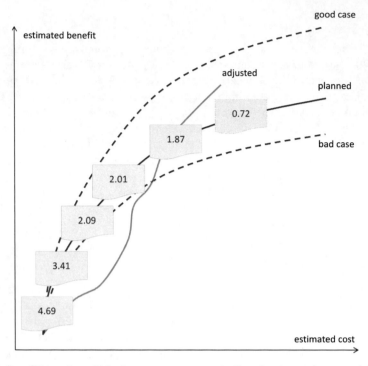

Fig. 2.4 Benefit/cost plan with bad-case, worst-case, and adjusted estimates (not to scale).

rather than 'story points'. Another reason for this choice, or change, of name is that there are other points to a story than what traditionally goes by the name *story point*, and those are, of course, benefit points.

The orange line in Fig. 2.4 is based on incremental experience, gained after developing and using functionality when increments are released. It is a recalculation of estimates based on that experience. Regarding benefit, stakeholder experience with the deployed product elements can alter the original perception of the life cycle benefit, thus leading to adjusted benefit estimates. Regarding cost, the actual cost of construction is known for the deployed product elements. The life cycle cost estimates can be adjusted accordingly; this is particularly easy in cases in which life cycle cost is computed as a proportion of the development cost [6]. We will revisit this topic in Chapter 3.

2.5   The Estimates in Time

The plan in Fig. 2.4 expresses the order in which product elements will be put into construction, in other words, when the potential benefit in the form of functionality

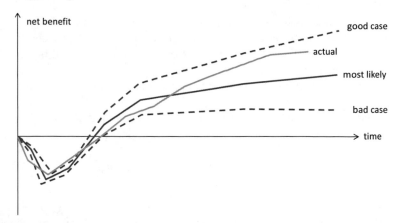

Fig. 2.5 Net benefit periodization plan, with the most likely, bad-case, worst-case, and adjusted estimates (not to scale).

will be constructed and at what life cycle cost. This figure is simply a productivity plan in terms of potential benefit and cost for use during incremental development.

To express the timeline in which cost is incurred and benefit is realized, a different visualization is needed. The blue solid line in Fig. 2.5 illustrates how net benefit could realize over time. In the beginning, product elements are sent into construction, with no other parts of this particular system in production, so there will be only costs and no benefit. Once the first release is deployed, benefit can slowly start to manifest itself, increasing as more product elements are completed and put into production. Technology uptake in the organization can take time, delaying the realization of the potential benefit constructed in the system. Eventually, however, net benefit breaks even and rises steadily as the system is adopted.

Chapter 7 will show how points-based estimates can be periodized to provide this kind of planning in terms of return on investment or net present value [3]. The points can again be instantiated with different monetary values that reflect the most likely scenario together with good- and bad-case scenarios, as illustrated by the dashed blue lines in Fig. 2.5. Retaining the product elements' relative estimates ensures that no re-estimation is necessary for the sake of contemplating different scenarios. The actual net benefit realization can then be plotted against the plan, as illustrated by the orange line in Fig. 2.5.

2.6 Setting the Stage

Sliger and Broderick [9] introduced the idea of the *agile fractal*, pointing out that a sequence of *planning, incremental development*, and *retrospective* should occur at all levels of project work. The fractal can naturally be extended upward to portfolios and strategic periods [5]. Figure 2.6 illustrates the idea: the enterprise, in a certain strategic period, finds that, to meet its goals, it must initiate an initiative, perhaps in the form of a portfolio of information technology development projects. Portfolio work is organized into individual projects. Project work is organized into releases, releases are organized into iterations, and iterations are organized in daily work, which consists of programming tasks. The agile fractal shows what is known as a *work breakdown structure*.

The methodological principles presented in this book apply at all levels. However, we will elaborate these principles at the four upper levels of the agile fractal, which covers projects and portfolios of projects. In the next chapter, we start with projects and will move on to portfolios in the following chapter.

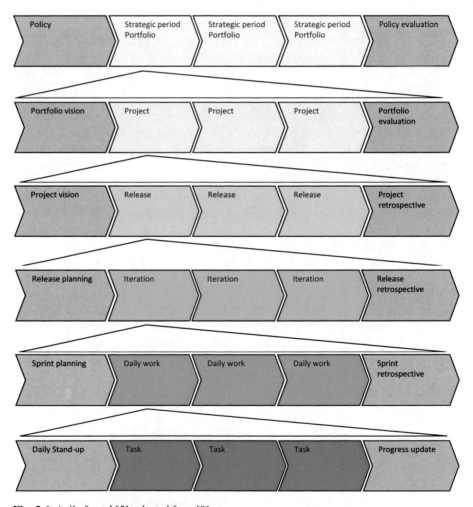

Fig. 2.6 Agile fractal [5], adapted from [9].

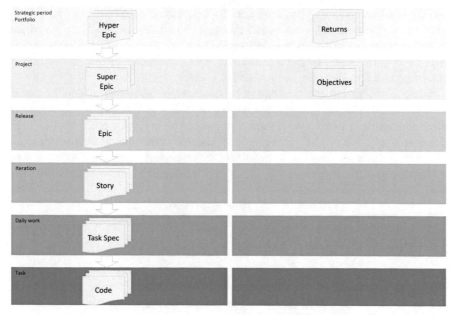

Fig. 2.7 Left: Product breakdown structure of product elements according to the agile fractal. Right: Associated benefit criteria.

2.7 Product Elements and Product Breakdown Structure

In modern development methodology, there is an explicit focus on customer value. To reflect this aspect, requirements are often formulated from the perspectives of users in so-called *user stories*. Actually, and more generally in today's projects, value concerns a range of stakeholders, from enterprise managers to system developers, deployers, and maintainers, and on to end users, society, and the general public in many cases. Accordingly, one could instead formulate *stakeholder stories* from the perspectives of these salient stakeholders.

Requirement specifications should reflect the current, always limited but evolving perception and knowledge of needs for the system, or systems, under development. Therefore, best practice suggests the stepwise elaboration and detailing of specifications as one gains knowledge and experience. Such elaboration and detailing result in what is commonly known as a *product breakdown structure*, where *product elements* are divided into finer-grained parts and elaborated and detailed. Figure 2.7 (left panel) shows a product breakdown structure according to the agile fractal in Fig. 2.6.

In agile management, abstract high-level user stories often go by the name of *epics*, while more detailed user stories are often called simply *stories*. In Fig. 2.7, we depict *hyper epics*, which describe the use cases for the entire portfolio from the point of view of relevant stakeholders at that level. These hyper epics are broken down in successive stages. When individual projects are defined, hyper epics are broken down into *super epics* that state the overall use cases for the project as a whole from the point of view of stakeholders at that level. Then, during project inception, (traditional) epics are declared. These are then distributed to releases. When a release is ready for construction, its epics are broken down into stories and, further, to task specifications, which lead to code.[2]

Stakeholder centricity means that stakeholder stories should partition functionality into parts that are meaningful to those stakeholders in terms of scope at a given stage. For viable benefits management, product elements at the epics levels should express integral, functionally meaningful, and deployable units of functionality that provide identifiable value for stakeholders. Such product elements go by several names, for example, minimum feature set, MVP [8], and minimum marketable feature [3, 4].

2.8   Benefit Criteria to Match

Figure 2.7 (right panel) shows the associated benefit criteria for the product breakdown structure. The benefit criteria for product elements at a given level are at the level above. Conceivably, there could be benefit criteria for hyper epics, and even higher levels of both product elements and benefit criteria, but the scope of the figure is sufficient for our discussion.

Note that there are benefit criteria for only epics and higher levels. This is because product elements at lower levels usually concern aspects of functionality that are too detailed to relate to benefit criteria (in a sense, they are below the minimum for an MVP). Product elements at these lower levels still need to be assigned benefit points. We will address how benefit points are relayed downward in due course.

Finally, the benefit criteria will themselves be assessed through higher-level benefit criteria. For the scope of our discussion, we will see that objectives are assessed on returns.

2.9*   A Note on Project Triangles

The iron triangle of project management (Fig. 2.8, leftmost panel) considers quality to be the result of balancing scope, schedule, and costs. In this context, quality is the technical build quality (intrinsic quality), whereas scope, within the meaning of 'functionality for the customer', is really the notion that is closest to benefit. One can have perfect intrinsic quality – no bugs and a perfect architecture – that fails to deliver the functionality requested.

The agile community has abandoned the iron triangle for the agile triangle (Fig. 2.8, middle panel). In the agile triangle, extrinsic quality or benefit, is an ex-

---

[2] In the project management tool Jira, the analogous product elements in the product breakdown structure are the *theme, initiative, epic, story, task,* and so forth.

Fig. 2.8 Project management triangles.

plicit factor, in recognition of the prime objective of delivering valuable software to the customer. The agile triangle distinguishes between intrinsic and extrinsic quality, and the factors of the iron triangle are viewed as constraints.

Although the iron and agile triangles aim to strike a balance between their factors, the explicit polarization makes it tempting to emphasize one factor over the others. We contend that benefit and cost should not be polarized, but, rather, integrated into a single metric. The benefit/cost triangle (Fig. 2.8, rightmost panel) therefore has the benefit-cost ratio as a factor. Again, quality refers to technical quality – including the architecture – and the scope and schedule are the remaining constraints. We are thus saying that one should maximize the benefit-cost ratio, subject to scope, schedule, and intrinsic quality.

Jørgensen [7] found the iron triangle factors (on time, on budget, and with a fixed specified functionality) to be poorly correlated to realized benefit. Not surprisingly, a focus on scope, that is, delivering the initially specified functionality, was found to be in conflict with success in delivering benefit. Instead, change in the scope in accordance with changing business needs and learning was found to be a strong indicator of success in delivering client benefits.

In our context, the iron triangle represents the traditional focus on cost control. This focus is inadvertently inherited in agile, for example, in the burndown chart tracking the amount of story points that are constructed relative to the plan. Figure 2.9 (leftmost panel) illustrates this focus for a planned constant burndown rate

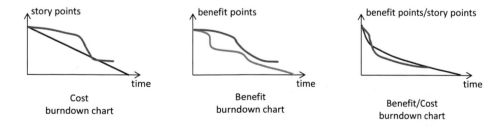

Fig. 2.9 Burndown charts for cost-driven development, benefit-driven development, and benefit/cost-driven development. The actual burndown lines are in orange.

of story points (red line), that is, assuming constant productivity, where the orange line denotes actual productivity.

With benefit points in place and in line with the explicit focus on benefit, the agile diagram could suggest focusing on the burndown of benefit points. Figure 2.9 (middle panel) illustrates this focus for a planned burndown rate of benefit points according to the construction of product elements with the largest amount of benefit points first (green line), given constant productivity. In a sense, this approach expresses the maximization of benefit at all costs, or the maximization of benefit within the bounds of fixed costs or a schedule.

In this book, we look at managing neither by cost alone nor by benefit alone; rather, we seek to maximize benefit relative to cost. In addition, we want to ensure that the most benefit/cost-worthy functionality is constructed and put into production first. The appropriate burndown is based on the ratio of benefit points to story points (Fig. 2.9, rightmost panel).

The implications can be that exceeding the budgeted cost can be acceptable if the estimates show that benefit will be generated that justify that cost, that is, if the benefit-cost ratio is sufficiently high. Equally relevant, it is acceptable to stop construction when the benefit-cost ratio falls below a certain level.

References

1. B.W. Boehm, *Software Engineering Economics*. Prentice Hall, 1981.
2. M. Cohn, *Agile Estimating and Planning*. Prentice Hall, 2005.
3. M. Denne and J. Cleland-Huang, *Software by Numbers: Low-Risk, High-Return Development*. Prentice Hall, 2003.
4. M. Denne and J. Cleland-Huang, "The incremental funding method: Data-driven software development," *IEEE Software*, vol. 21, no. 3, pp. 39–47, May/June 2004.
5. J.E. Hannay, K. Brathen, and O.M. Mevassvik, "Agile requirements handling in a service-oriented taxonomy of capabilities," *Requirements Engineering*, vol. 22, no. 2, pp. 289–314, 2017.
6. C. Jones, *Estimating Software Costs: Bringing Realism to Estimating*, 2nd ed. McGraw-Hill, 2007.
7. M. Jørgensen, "A survey of the characteristics of projects with success in delivering client benefits," *Information and Software Technology*, vol. 78, pp. 83–94, 2016.
8. V. Lenarduzzi and D. Taibi, "MVP explained: A systematic mapping study on the definitions of Minimal Viable Product," in *2016 42th Euromicro Conference on Software Engineering and Advanced Applications (SEAA)*, Aug 2016, pp. 112–119.
9. M. Sliger and S. Broderick, *The Software Project Manager's Bridge to Agility*. Addison Wesley, 2008.

Chapter 3
Benefit Points for the Project

> Vision without action is a dream. Action without vision is simply passing the time. Action with vision is making a positive difference.

JOEL BARKER

Abstract We start by looking at projects and their most abstract product elements, the epics, and show how to estimate their benefit using benefit points. Then we show how to sort epics according to a benefit-cost index to help decide the order in which to put epics into releases. Instantiating points with a monetary value provides added means of prioritizing and determining when to stop sending epics into construction. We show two modes of estimating benefit: one where the purpose is to fulfil a given goal (confirmatory mode), and the other where the purpose is to explore where to set the goal (exploratory mode).

3.1 Overview

In a development project, *product elements* are represented by requirements specifications in some form, such as user stories. The *benefit criteria* (Fig. 2.1) are then given by *project objectives*. Project objectives express the organization's reasons for initiating the development project in the first place. The purpose of the project is to fulfil these objectives.

Figure 3.1 shows a project as part of the agile fractal (Fig. 2.6), with its high-level requirements specifications in the form of epics. At this stage, the epics are to be assessed on project objectives and have not yet been distributed to project releases. The epics' benefits are estimated according to their assessed contribution to the objectives. This is the *effect* relation in Fig. 3.1. The system under development is expected to have an impact on business processes. This impact is effected through the system's functionality, designed with the intent to enable users and other systems to perform tasks in an overall better or more efficient manner.

The project objectives are, in turn, assessed on planned returns. This is the *worth* relation in Fig. 3.1. The worth relation has nothing to do with the system's functionality. Rather, the relation expresses the expected gain in value the objectives imply, once they are fulfilled.

J. E. Hannay, *Benefit/Cost-Driven Agile Software Development*,
Simula SpringerBriefs on Computing 8,
https://doi.org/10.1007/978-3-030-74218-8_3

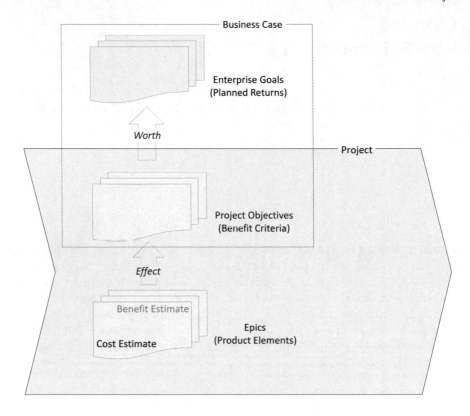

Fig. 3.1 A project has specific objectives. An epic's *effect* is assessed in terms of its contribution to the objectives. Objectives have different *worth* in terms of their contributions to planned returns. We state that *benefit = effect × worth*.

Then, *benefit = effect × worth*; that is, the benefit of an epic is its effect on project objectives times the objectives' worth in returns. Assessing *effect* and assessing *worth* are fundamentally different tasks, and we make a point of assessing these two relations one at a time. Indeed, the two assessments can be made by different stakeholder groups, and carried out in any sequence or in parallel. One should not attempt to combine the two assessments into one. Assessing the effects of epics on objectives, while simultaneously adjusting for the various objectives' worth exceeds most people's cognitive capacity. Because projects usually lack conceptual clarity when it comes to benefits management, projects often end up assessing benefit in a way that effectively combines and collapses these two steps.

Figure 3.2 (bottom portion) shows examples of epics in a development project for a public service organization.

Product elements can also be expressed in terms of related notions such as *minimum viable change* and *minimum viable transformation*, which emphasize the change in business processes induced by product elements.

Case 4. An internal revenue administration recently implemented changes to the way salary information is registered, processed, and reported. Since this involved substantial alterations to end-user processes and internal data processing, the product owner decided to deploy rather quickly the simplest possible version of the new web-based functionality to users in a limited region with uncomplicated life and work situations, in other words, a minimal viable change. This piece of meaningful functionality providing immediate benefit allowed the project to learn early from a low-risk real-life deployment. After that, further functionality was rolled out to successively larger portions of the population.

Returns:
Ret1: Reduced number of man-hours
Ret2: Reduced number of compensations
Ret3: Improved public image of the organization

Objectives:
Obj1: Reduce average case processing time by 30%
Obj2: Reduce number of wrong case decisions by 90%
Obj3: Reduce the average interaction time between the applicant and the application processor by 70%

Epics:
E1: *As* an applicant *I can* secure my identity in the application process *by using* MyID module *to* authenticate myself
E2: *As* an applicant *I can* increase speed & accuracy of the application process *by using* MyID module *to* autofill personal data
E3: *As* a case processor *I can* find all relevant information for a case *by using* the Cross Search module *to* retrieve applicant information from all relevant and permissible data sources in a single search
E4: *As* a case processor *I can* receive alerts when deadlines are approaching *by using* the Reports module *to* finish cases on time and avoid complaints
E5: *As* a case processor *I can* view graphical trends over cases per status *by using* the Reports module *to* increase planning and motivation
E6: *As* a division manager *I can* manage my division's productivity *by using* the Reports module *to* view statistics to monitor the time and quality of case processing
E7: *As* a returning applicant *I can* obtain an overview of earlier applications *by using* the Reports module *to* obtain an overview of my history with the public sector
E8: ...
...

Fig. 3.2 Example of epics, objectives, and returns (public sector).

3.2 Project Objectives

A project should have designated *objectives* that express the project's intended effects on the organization's business processes. Figure 3.2 (middle portion) shows examples of objectives in a development project for a public service organization.

We will present two modes of benefit estimation. One mode is where the objectives are set that the project must fulfil. We call this the *confirmatory mode*. The other mode is where stakeholders try to determine what the project will be able to deliver on the given objectives. We call this the *exploratory mode*. As with all top-down and bottom-up tactics, it is sensible to combine the two modes in an interleaving manner, especially in an environment geared to project learning and adaptation.

We will explain the principles of benefit estimation for the confirmatory mode, because things are simpler in that mode. Then, we will explain how to estimate benefit in the exploratory mode.

3.3 Effect Points: Benefit Points for the Effect Relation

For the effect relation, benefit estimates are assigned to epics according to how much each epic is perceived to contribute to objectives, in terms of relative benefit points. For the effect relation, benefit points are called *effect benefit points*, or *effect points* for short.

Since there are several objectives, the assignment of effect points is more complex than assigning story points for cost. Figure 3.3 shows a table with effect points for eight epics assessed on three objectives. As a rule, all epics should be assessed on one objective before moving to the next, as indicated by the vertical lines in Fig. 3.3. This is because objectives can have different metrics (time, money, quality, etc.), and special attention is required to perform relative assessments across metrics.

	Obj1	Obj2	Obj3	Total
E1	16	8	12	36
E2	25	35	8	68
E3	25	4	7	36
E4	10	13	3	26
E5	1	5	31	37
E6	6	9	8	23
E7	15	13	12	40
E8	2	13	19	34
Total	100	100	100	300

Fig. 3.3 Effect benefit points (effect points) assigned by distributing 100 points per objective. Benefit points provided by the stakeholder group are shown on a white background. The totals in the shaded area are computed automatically by your tool.

In this example, stakeholders have used a technique in which they distribute 100 linear points for an objective over the epics. This *parts of the whole* technique is suitable in the confirmatory mode: 100 points represent an objective's complete fulfilment, and they can be distributed among epics according to their relative contributions. You can also use open-ended scales, such as the Fibonacci sequence familiar from planning poker, in the confirmatory mode, but the calculations are slightly more complicated. Consult Section 3.13 on this topic later.

It is essential that you only concentrate on the effect relation at this stage: do not be concerned with the fact that objectives can represent different levels of worth! That consideration belongs to a different exercise, which we will address shortly. For more on the technique of assigning benefit points, read about *benefit poker* in Section 3.15, and find out more on the issue of *multiple objectives* in Section 3.16.

3.4 Planned Returns

Having explicit, preferably measurable objectives for one's project is one of many signs of organizational maturity. The assignment of benefit points to product elements in terms of those objectives is a first step to handling a project's generation of business value.

However, the project objectives represent the project's estimated effects, and therefore coexist for the duration of the project. To link the project to the organization's long-term goals, one must link project objectives to the business return, as planned in strategic goals. For example, a planned return for the public service organization example above could involve the goals in Fig. 3.2 (top portion).

3.5 Worth Points: Benefit Points for the Worth Relation

A project's objectives, once fulfilled, are expected to yield various degrees of return for the enterprise. This is the worth relation. *Worth benefit points* (or *worth points*) are used to express estimates of worth. The benefit criteria (Fig. 2.1) are then the planned returns above. Figure 3.4 exemplifies the technique of distributing 100 points per return: reaching *Obj3* is assessed to yield on *Ret1* as much as the two other objectives combined (see the *Ret1* column in Fig. 3.4).

For the public service example, this means that stakeholders assess that a 70% reduction in the average interaction time between the applicant and the application processor will reduce man-hours to the same extent as reaching the other two objectives together.

Returns are outside a project's domain of argument, and the project assumes the goals expressed in returns as given. For the project, the worth relation is therefore confirmatory, by definition. When we discuss portfolios in Chapter 4, we will see the worth relation in an exploratory mode as well.

	Ret1	Ret2	Ret3
Obj1	25	29	33
Obj2	25	43	40
Obj3	50	29	27
Total	100	100	100

Fig. 3.4 Worth benefit points (worth points) produced from distributing 100 points per return. Benefit points provided by the stakeholder group are shown against a white background. The totals and weights in the shaded area can be computed automatically by your tool.

Again, techniques such as the distribution of 100 points are suitable in the confirmatory mode. For the worth relations, this implies that one plans for the project's objectives to fulfil the returns entirely; in other words, the returns represent exactly the expected business value of the project. A planned return, say, *Reduced number of man-hours*, could be a strategic goal spanning several projects, initiatives, and programmes in an enterprise, but, here, only the part of the return that the project is expected to fulfil is considered.

3.6 Monetary Returns

Effect points represent estimates of the system's effect on business processes, and worth points represent the return in terms of strategic goals from changing those business processes. Both effect points and worth points are relative assessments. In particular, worth points express the relative degree to which project objectives contribute to returns. If one now estimates a project's returns in monetary terms, one can determine the project's estimated monetary benefit. Project returns can also pose as a strategic management goal, further emphasizing the confirmatory mode.

Suppose, then, that project stakeholders and strategic management assess that the project objectives, once fulfilled, will yield monetary returns as follows: *Ret1*, 40 million; *Ret2*, 14 million; and *Ret3*, 22.5 million. The objectives' worth points then imply that the project's objectives *Obj1*, *Obj2*, and *Obj3* are estimated to contribute

	Ret1	Ret2	Ret3		Weight
million:	40	14	22.5	Total	Project
Obj1	25	29	33	21.50	0.28
Obj2	25	43	40	25.00	0.33
Obj3	50	29	27	30.00	0.39
Total	100	100	100	76.50	1.00

Fig. 3.5 Returns are given monetary value (in millions of one's favourite currency). For each objective, one calculates the column denoted 'Total', by multiplying the monetary values by the objective's expected proportions of contribution and summing the results. For example, for *Obj1*, we obtain (40 * 0.25) + (14 * 0.29) + (22.5 * 0.33) = 21.50.

21.5 million, 25 million, and 30 million, respectively, to the total of 76.5 million (the 'Total' column in Fig. 3.5). Thus, the project's objectives, once fulfilled, contribute unevenly to the project's return. This is due to objectives contributing differently to returns, as expressed in their worth points, together with the different estimated worth of the project returns.

3.7   Balanced Effect Points

The fact that some project objectives are worth more than others must be reflected in the way the project prioritizes the backlog.

The 'Weight' column in Fig. 3.5 shows the weights of the objectives according to their contribution to returns. When objectives contribute unevenly to returns, a benefit point with respect to one objective will represent a different unit of benefit than a benefit point given with respect to another objective. To keep things manageable, we balance the number of benefit points so that a benefit point always represents the same amount of benefit, regardless of the objective.

Quite simply, multiply the effect points for an epic by the relevant objective's weight; for epic $E1$ on $Obj1$, $16*0.28=4.48$. We can then define a *balance* function as

$$\text{balance}(BP_p, w_c) = BP_p * w_c \tag{3.1}$$

where BP_p is the number of benefit points for product element p, and weight w_c is the weight of criterion c. So if BP_{ij} is the number of benefit points for epic i on objective j and w_j is the weight of objective j, the general formula for balancing effect points is

$$\text{balance}(BP_{ij}, w_j) = BP_{ij} * w_j \tag{3.2}$$

Figure 3.6 shows the resulting balanced benefit points for our example.

	Obj1	Obj2	Obj3	
Weights:	0.28	0.33	0.39	Total
E1	4.48	2.64	4.68	11.80
E2	7.00	11.55	3.12	21.67
E3	7.00	1.32	2.73	11.05
E4	2.80	4.29	1.17	8.26
E5	0.28	1.65	12.09	14.02
E6	1.68	2.97	3.12	7.77
E7	4.20	4.29	4.68	13.17
E8	0.56	4.29	7.41	12.26
Total	28.00	33.00	39.00	100

Fig. 3.6 Effect points, balanced according to the worth of objectives.

	Obj1	Obj2	Obj3	
Weights:	0.28	0.33	0.39	Total
E1	13.44	7.92	14.04	35.40
E2	21.00	34.65	9.36	65.01
E3	21.00	3.96	8.19	33.15
E4	8.40	12.87	3.51	24.78
E5	0.84	4.95	36.27	42.06
E6	5.04	8.91	9.36	23.31
E7	12.60	12.87	14.04	39.51
E8	1.68	12.87	22.23	36.78
Total	84.00	99.00	117.00	300

Fig. 3.7 Effect points balanced according to the worth of objectives and normalized to 300 points in total.

If you want to keep the total number of effect points in the project (300 in this example) constant in your tables (for cosmetic reasons), you can multiply by the ratio of the desired total number of benefit points (300 here) by the current total number of benefit points (100 here); for epic $E1$ on $Obj1$, 16*0.28 * 300/100 = 13.44. We can define a *normalize* function as follows:

$$\text{normalize}(BP_p, BP_{\text{desired total}}, BP_{\text{total}}) = BP_p * (BP_{\text{desired total}}/BP_{\text{total}}) \quad (3.3)$$

where BP_p is the number of benefit points for product element p, $BP_{\text{desired total}}$ is the desired total amount of benefit points, and BP_{total} is the current total amount of benefit points. Thus, the formula for normalizing the amount of balanced effect points $b_{i,j} = \text{balance}(BP_{ij}, w_j)$ for epic i on objective j is

$$\text{normalize}(b_{ij}, BP_{\text{desired total}}/BP_{\text{balanced total}}) \quad (3.4)$$

where $BP_{\text{balanced total}}$ is the total number of effect points after balancing.

Balancing and normalizing should be carried out automatically in your spreadsheet or project management tool. Figure 3.7 presents the resulting normalized balanced benefit points for our example, where keeping the total amount of benefit points (300) illustrates how the original points in Fig. 3.3 are redistributed according to the objectives' worth.

3.8 Cost Estimates: Size Points

Story points are routinely assigned for estimating cost in projects, and we assume procedures for doing this, such as planning poker, are known. However, we will make a few remarks in the context of benefit/cost management.

Benefit manifests itself after deployment; therefore, to obtain a sensible benefit-cost measure, the cost estimates should include post-deployment costs in addition to

	SP
E1	8
E2	8
E3	3
E4	5
E5	13
E6	13
E7	5
E8	8
Total	63

Fig. 3.8 Size points (SP).

development costs. We will use *size points* for this. Traditionally, story points reflect development cost only. However, life cycle cost is often assumed to be proportional to, or linearly dependent on, development cost (for more details, see Section 3.17 and e.g. [27]). Under that assumption, size points can be assigned if they are story points, since the relative proportions between story points remain the same for development and life cycle costs. Our methods apply, regardless of that assumption. However, under that assumption (and when it is warranted), some of the methods can take on a simpler form. In any event, for our running example, we assume the size points presented in Fig. 3.8.

3.9 Benefit-Cost Index

One can now immediately calculate the benefit point-to-size point ratio in Fig. 3.9 (left) to obtain a relative benefit-cost measure. The effect points are obtained from Fig. 3.7, and the size points are from Fig. 3.8. Size points can be divided by benefit

	BP	SP	BP/SP
E1	35.40	8	4.43
E2	65.01	8	8.13
E3	33.15	3	11.05
E4	24.78	5	4.96
E5	42.06	13	3.24
E6	23.31	13	1.79
E7	39.51	5	7.90
E8	36.78	8	4.60
Total	300	63	4.76

	BP	SP	BP/SP
E3	33.15	3	11.05
E2	65.01	8	8.13
E7	39.51	5	7.90
E4	24.78	5	4.96
E8	36.78	8	4.60
E1	35.40	8	4.43
E5	42.06	13	3.24
E6	23.31	13	1.79
Total	300	63	4.76

Fig. 3.9 Benefit-cost index. The ratios (BP/SP) of effect benefit points (BP) to size points (SP) are presented in the left panel, and sorted in descending order in the right panel.

points because both types of points are on a so-called *ratio scale*[1]. It is common
to use nominal schemes – such as MoSCoW [25], which produces four categories
of importance (textitMust have, *Should have*, *Could have*, and *Won't have*) – to
assess benefit. In that case, benefit estimates cannot be divided by cost. To obtain
a benefit-to-cost measure from MoSCoW, one could order the product elements
by increasing cost within each category and then order the backlog by selecting
the ordered elements in the Must have, then Should have, Could have, and Won't
have categories. However, it is entirely possible for an element in a less important
category to have a higher benefit-cost ratio than a given element in a more important
category, due to low cost. Without a sound measure of benefit-cost provided by ratio
scales, one would not become aware of such incidents.

There are several useful things that can be done with a benefit-cost index. If one
wanted to realize maximum benefit relative to cost early, one would consider putting
epic *E3* into construction first. Figure. 3.9 (right panel) shows the sorted epics, with
those with the highest benefit-cost index at the top. We will investigate this and other
ways to use benefit/cost estimates in later chapters.

3.10   Instantiating Points with Money

Points-based estimates are relative estimates, where monetary value is abstracted
away. Practice and research suggest that it is easier to perform comparative judgements (one is larger than the other), rather than judgements on spot values.

An additional, powerful aspect of using relative sizes, such as benefit points and
size points, is that one can assign actual monetary values to points, according to

	Benefit	Cost	Benefit/Cost
E3	8.45	1.80	4.70
E2	16.58	4.80	3.45
E7	10.08	3.00	3.36
E4	6.32	3.00	2.11
E8	9.38	4.80	1.95
E1	9.03	4.80	1.88
E5	10.73	7.80	1.38
E6	5.94	7.80	0.76
Total	76.50	37.80	2.02

Fig. 3.10 Benefit/cost. The same as Figure. 3.9 (right panel), but with effect points instantiated at
1 BP = 0.255 million and size points instantiated at 1 SP = 0.6 million.

---

[1] Scales come in several flavours. A *nominal* scale categorizes items by name, with no ordering. An
ordinal scale puts on ordering on items, without stating distances between them. An *interval* scale
orders items with fixed distances; two items classified as a '1' and a '2' have the same difference in
magnitude as two items classified as a '2' and a '3', but a '4' is not double that of a '2' (examples
are the Celsius and Fahrenheit temperature scales. A *ratio* scale has a defined zero point, which
enables multiplication and division.

current knowledge. Figure 3.10 shows the results of Figure 3.9 with effect points instantiated at 1 BP = 0.225 million and 1 SP = 0.6 million. The monetary value (0.225 million) of an effect point is set by dividing the total benefit budget (76.50 million) by the number of effect points assigned to the project (300 BP). [2] The monetary value representing the life cycle cost of a size point is set at 0.6 million, say, based on structured stakeholder meetings and past experience from earlier projects with similar characteristics. For example, structured discussions could have established the development cost of a size point at 0.3 million. Then a linear model of post-deployment costs might suggest that the life cycle cost is twice the development cost. Thus, the life cycle cost estimate is 37.8 million, and the life cycle benefit estimate is 76.5 million. For this example, these values could be the initial estimates for the business case, prior to project learning. However, one can instantiate points with alternative values that reflect an initiative's current understanding or different scenarios. We will see this practice in action later.

With monetary values, benefit and cost have the same denomination. With the values set as above, it is evident that, according to initial estimates, epic *E6* has a benefit-cost ratio below one, which means that this epic, as a whole, should not be put into construction, since it will return less benefit than it will cost. Depending on a project's expectation levels and the level of risk the project is willing to take on, one might want to look out for *E5* as well. Its expected benefit is only about 40% more than its cost. Thus, benefit-cost deliberations can help one decide not only the order in which to construct product elements, but also when to stop construction.

3.11 Soft Returns

Return *Ret3* in the example in Fig. 3.2 is a typical qualitative, or 'soft', return. It does not directly refer to quantifiable measures. Since qualitative returns could be an essential part of business value, it is important to be able to include them in our scheme. Another example could be *Ret4: increased information infrastructure capability in society*. Such expected returns could be more important than quantitative financial ones, for example, in terms of political justification for initiating a development project or in terms of environmental and ethical sustainability goals.

The problem is that such returns can be very hard to quantify. Sometimes explicit quantification in terms of the monetary value of qualitative returns is required by law, such as in government-funded development projects, where there are obligations to follow socioeconomic models for the analysis of societal benefit. However, insisting on the hard quantification of qualitative values could be perceived as practically impossible and lead to the omission of such returns. In line with satisficing rather than optimization [44] and simplicity, we propose a method for implicitly quantifying soft returns, the *model for integrating soft and hard returns on invest-*

---

[2] In Section 4.3, we will discuss how one might set the total benefit budget.

ment, or *MISHRI*. The idea is the same as that presented by [5] for a slightly different context . So, how did we assess that return to be worth 22.5 million?

The entire methodology in this book is based on small steps that can be overcome by human cognitive resources. The required expert estimations are based on relative comparison, which is also what we recommend to quantify qualitative returns. For this, one needs to fix the value of at least one return, say, *Ret1*. One can now ask how important *Ret3* is relative to *Ret1*. If it is equally important, its monetary value should be set at 40 million; if it is less important, the same question can be asked relative to *Ret2*. One could also determine that *Ret3* is more important than *Ret2*, but closer to *Ret2* than to *Ret1* by, say, 10%, which implies a monetary value of 22.5 million. In other words, the quantitative returns can be used as markers for comparing qualitative returns.

Relevant stakeholders should be involved in this process, and one can use similar techniques as for the other expert estimates in our approach.

This inclusion of soft returns means that one can take into account their influence on project objectives. Soft returns will thus influence the backlog order. Later, one can choose whether to include soft returns in the actual return calculations. This might not always be appropriate, because there will not necessarily be any actual cash flow from soft returns. We leave that discussion for later. It is easy to include and exclude soft returns (and compare their effects). For *Ret3*, we simply set its value to zero and determine how the automatic calculations in your tool change. Figure 3.11 shows how not considering *Ret3* produces a different distribution of effect points on the epics, and therefore different ordering in terms of the benefit-cost index.

The relativistic approach to integrating soft returns above is designed to be non-intrusive in daily work as a simple, good-enough approach to an inherently difficult problem. In contrast, there are comprehensive approaches to quantifying planned returns that are far more elaborate, such as that of [14], but they will require a great deal of effort. One should be aware of both approaches.

	BP	SP	BP/SP
E3	32.34	3	10.78
E7	39.24	5	7.85
E2	61.56	8	7.70
E8	38.34	8	4.79
E4	23.46	5	4.69
E1	35.52	8	4.44
E5	46.20	13	3.55
E6	23.34	13	1.80
Total	300	63	4.76

Fig. 3.11 The benefit-cost index when *Ret3* is not taken into account. Compared to Fig. 3.9, *E7* and *E2* have changed places, as have *E4* and *E8*.

	Obj1	Obj2	Obj3	Total
E1	13	5	8	26
E2	21	21	5	47
E3	21	2	5	28
E4	8	8	2	18
E5	1	3	21	25
E6	5	5	5	15
E7	13	8	8	29
E8	2	8	13	23
Total	84	60	67	211

Fig. 3.12 Effect points obtained by assigning numbers from the Fibonacci sequence.

3.12 Effect Points in the Exploratory Mode

We have illustrated the main idea of benefit points using the technique of distributing a fixed number of points (100 in the examples). An alternative is to use open-ended scales, where one assigns points without assuming that the sum must be a certain number.

If you are familiar with planning poker, chances are that you will have used Fibonacci numbers to assign story points in an open-ended fashion. You can use the Fibonacci sequence for benefit points as well, and in this section, we will quickly go through the same steps as above to assign effect points, but now using the Fibonacci sequence in an open-ended fashion. It is possible to use the Fibonacci sequence as a fixed scale as well, and there will be examples of that later. Figure 3.12 shows our example with eight epics and three objectives, where numbers from the Fibonacci sequence have been used to assign the effect points. Again, epics are assessed against one objective at a time.

Whereas the technique of distributing 100 points prompts one to conduct an assessment relative to the total (100), using open-ended scales puts more emphasis on the direct relative assessment between items. The reason is that there is no global target (the upper bound of 100) to relate to. So, in the example, epic *E1* has been estimated to contribute substantially less than *E2* and *E3* to objective *Obj1*, but substantially more than *E4* and equally to *E7*. For objective *Obj2*, epic *E4* is assessed to contribute as much as *E5* and *E6* combined.

Now, since the scale is open ended, the effect point totals for the objectives may very well differ, as it does in Figure 3.12. This result can be interpreted in two ways: (A) the differences are an artefact of the estimation method or (B) the differences reflect a perception that the objectives are fulfilled to different degrees.

In the exploratory mode, (B) is the relevant interpretation.[3] There are various ways in which the project could be in an exploratory mode. We will mention a few possibilities.

---

[3] For interpretation (A), see Section 3.13.

3.12.1 Exploring the Effect of Epics

The project may want to determine what it can realistically achieve in terms of given objectives. For example, if the total number of effect points for an objective is substantially lower than for the other objectives, this could indicate that the stakeholder group thinks the epics do not have the potential to fulfil that objective to the full extent stated. This should prompt the project to re-evaluate the epics and perhaps redesign them so that they do fulfil the objectives.

3.12.2 Exploring the Feasibility of Objectives

The project, in the exploratory mode, could also start questioning the objectives themselves. This would initiate a discussion with the stakeholders responsible for defining project objectives.

Case 5. A new web-based customer solution was to be developed in an organization that provides services for handling intellectual property rights. Epics were specified and benefit estimated using planning poker cards. The resulting effect points under each objective (prior to normalization) differed to such a degree that the project leader questioned whether the benefit estimation group thought the system under development would be able to fulfil the planned objectives. The objectives were therefore revised, and benefit estimation reinitiated.

A more deliberate use of the exploratory mode than the one above would be to assess the epics' benefit with the explicit intent to determine the effects of the planned system. This would amount to exploring and determining what the objectives should realistically be, rather than setting objectives at the outset, as in the confirmatory mode. In such a case, one could start with rudimentary objective formulations, such as 'Reduce wrongful payments', without specifying by how much. The group of stakeholders can use effect points in benefit poker sessions as a means to discuss the effects of epics and eventually arrive at concrete objectives, such as 'Reduce wrongful payments by 70%'.

3.12.3 Working in the Exploratory Mode

In the exploratory mode, brainstorming-type discussions can be useful. To inform the discussion, effect point assessments can be used informally to reveal stakeholders' perceptions of the effect of epics or the viability of the objectives.

	Obj1	Obj2	Obj3	
Weights:	0.28	0.33	0.39	Total
E1	11.09	4.96	9.53	25.58
E2	17.92	20.84	5.95	44.71
E3	17.92	1.98	5.95	25.86
E4	6.83	7.94	2.38	17.15
E5	0.85	2.98	25.01	28.84
E6	4.27	4.96	5.95	15.18
E7	11.09	7.94	9.53	28.56
E8	1.71	7.94	15.48	25.12
Total	71.68	59.54	79.78	211

Fig. 3.13 Effect points obtained by assigning numbers from the Fibonacci sequence.

However, it is also possible to prioritize backlogs and, indeed, use all the other techniques in this book in the exploratory mode. Figure 3.13 shows the effect points from Table 3.12 balanced according to the objectives' worth, using Equation (3.2), and normalized to a total of 211 points, using Equation (3.4). The different objective totals indicate (under interpretation B) that the objectives are fulfilled to different degrees. Note that, here, the objectives' worth and returns are given in a confirmatory mode. In other words, the objectives are assumed to fulfil the returns in full, and the monetary value of worth points is also given, but the degree of the epics' fulfilment of objectives is under exploration and the monetary value of effect points is also unknown.[4]

3.12.4 Partial Fulfilment of Objectives

It could also be the case that one's project is not presented with project-specific objectives, but, instead, more general objectives. Then, the intention is not the project's total fulfilment of objectives. In this case, Figs. 3.12 and 3.13 express the epics' partial fulfilment of objectives.

However, when open-ended scales, such as the Fibonacci sequence, are used, the semantics for partial fulfilment are not obvious. For example, in Fig. 3.13, one would have to fix the fulfilment degree for at least one of the totals. For example, if we manage to determine that $Obj2$ is $x\%$ fulfilled by its approximately 60 effect points, we can calculate the remaining degree of fulfilment for the other objectives; if Obj_i has a total of BP_i effect points, its degree of fulfilment is approximately $BP_i/60 * x\%$. Alternatively, the absolute value of an effect point could be given. This can be the case if, after some time, organizations settle on conventions analogous to those in planning poker for cost estimation: through extended experience [7], stakeholders can recognize a product element as, for example, a typical five or a two. In other words, benefit point amounts become universal quantities applicable across projects

---

[4] We will look at *worth* points in the exploratory mode in the next chapter.

in or, perhaps, even across organizations. In that case, the degree of fulfilment is given directly by the effect point total of an objective relative to the objective's total worth points, which expresses its worth when totally fulfilled.

3.12.5   Closed Scales in the Exploratory Mode

If the intention is, indeed, the partial fulfilment of objectives, then using a *parts of the whole* assessment (distributing 100 points, say) could be easier than using open-ended scales, such as the Fibonacci scale. In that case, one would have to use an absolute assessment rather than a relative assessment: one would still distribute points from a pool of, say, 100 points among the epics, but one would have to evaluate each epic's absolute contribution to the objective. If an objective then receives a total of, for example, 44 points of 100, this would presumably indicate a fulfilment of 44% of that objective by the project's epics.

3.12.6   Ending Up in the Confirmatory Mode

In practice, a smooth combination of the exploratory and confirmatory modes is likely the most sensible. At the end of such a process, project objectives should arise that are to be met in full by the system under development. In other words, the exploratory mode should result in epics and objectives that the project addresses in the confirmatory mode.

We also promote the use of project-specific objectives and the semantics of total fulfilment. Even when provided objectives that are not project specific, one can derive project-specific objectives by determining what part of the general objectives the project will actually fulfil.

A common argument in favour of objectives not being specific to a project is that benefit occurs through synergy between multiple projects. This is, of course, true, and it is a good thing to acknowledge potential dependencies and the importance of a holistic perspective. However, it is also important to be able to express the benefit of each part. This is crucial for and at the heart of thinking in terms of minimum viable products (MVPs). MVPs are supposed to yield integral benefit, and that integral benefit should be asserted. The project is an organizational unit, and it is necessary to assert what that unit is capable of in terms of the benefit of its MVPs alone. Synergies with other projects' MVPs are the business of portfolio management, which is the topic of the next chapter.

	Obj1	Obj2	Obj3	Total
E1	10.88	5.86	8.40	25.14
E2	17.58	24.62	5.25	47.45
E3	17.58	2.34	5.25	25.18
E4	6.70	9.38	2.10	18.18
E5	0.84	3.52	22.04	26.40
E6	4.19	5.86	5.25	15.30
E7	10.88	9.38	8.40	28.66
E8	1.67	9.38	13.65	24.70
Total	70.33	70.33	70.33	211

Fig. 3.14 Effect points equalized for the total fulfilment of objectives (and normalized to 211 points in total). The points are automatically computed by your tool.

3.13 The Confirmatory Mode with Open-Ended Effect Points

Finally, it is, of course, possible to use open-ended scales in the confirmatory mode. This is highly relevant to projects whose participants are already accustomed to using the Fibonacci numbers for cost estimation. If the intention is to estimate in the confirmatory mode, then differences in effect point totals per objective must be viewed as an artefact of the estimation process (interpretation A above): when not distributing parts of the whole, it is generally hard and distracting for stakeholders to ensure equal benefit totals in the end.

To neutralize this unintended difference, we simply equalize the benefit points so that the objective totals are equal, that is, we divide by the total number of benefit points for the objective. For example, the equalized benefit points for $E1$ on $Obj1$ in Fig. 3.12 are 13/84 = 0.15. We define the following *equalize* function:

$$\text{equalize}(BP_{pc}, BP_c) = BP_{pc}/BP_c \qquad (3.5)$$

where BP_{pc} is the number of benefit points for product element p on benefit criterion c, and BP_c is the total number of benefit points on criterion c. So, if BP_{ij} is the number of effect points for epic i on objective j and BP_j is the total amount of effect points on objective j, then the formula for equalizing effect points is

$$\text{equalize}(BP_{ij}, BP_j) = BP_{ij}/BP_j \qquad (3.6)$$

Figure 3.14 shows the effect points of our example equalized. The points are also normalized to 211 points in total by normalize($e_{ij}, 211, BP_{\text{equalized total}}$ for $e_{ij} =$ equalize(BP_{ij}, BP_j), where $BP_{\text{equalized total}}$) is the total number of effect points after equalizing.

Then, Fig. 3.15 shows the balanced and normalized effect points for our example, using Equation (3.4).

Therefore, Fig. 3.16 (left panel) shows the epics sorted as in Fig. 3.9, but now with Fibonacci-based effect points. Figure 3.16 (right panel) has effect points instantiated at 1 BP = 0.36 million and 1 SP = 0.6 million. With 211 total effect points, the amount per effect point is different than in Section 3.10, where the total number of effect points was 300.

We can also compare Figs. 3.16 and 3.10. The values are comparable, but not equal. The differences are an artefact of using two different scales.

3.14   To Sum Up...

We have introduced benefit points for epics, called effect points. We have also introduced benefit points for objectives, called worth points. Using simple methods, you can assign benefit points based on a project's business case, using stakeholder knowledge and project expertise. This comprises a *core practice* alongside story point, or size point, estimation. Now, since you can assign both cost and benefit estimates to your product elements, you have the basics to monitor and learn from your project, to work towards generating as much benefit as possible, in addition to controlling cost.

A key feature to this core practice is a loosely coupled approach that allows a focus on one relation at a time. You are to focus on the relation between epics and objectives, disregarding the relation between objectives and returns, and to focus on the relation between objectives and returns, without having to think about epics. The combination of your assessments of the two relations can, and should, be generated automatically by the project management tool the project is using.

In contrast, assessing an epic's contribution to an objective while taking into account that objective's contribution to various returns and reflecting all this in the number of benefit points for the epic is hard. Trying to do all of that for several objectives is close to impossible. Yet, in practice, this is precisely what projects set out to do; not deliberately, but because they lack clear concept of benefit. For similar reasons, it is important to clearly delineate cost and benefit as separate concerns

	Obj1	Obj2	Obj3	
Weights:	0.28	0.33	0.39	Total
E1	9.18	5.75	9.88	24.80
E2	14.83	24.13	6.18	45.13
E3	14.83	2.30	6.18	23.30
E4	5.65	9.19	2.47	17.31
E5	0.71	3.45	25.94	30.09
E6	3.53	5.75	6.18	15.45
E7	9.18	9.19	9.88	28.25
E8	1.41	9.19	16.06	26.66
Total	59.30	68.95	82.75	211

Fig. 3.15 Effect points equalized for the total fulfilment of objectives and balanced against the objectives' worth (and normalized to 211 points in total). The points are automatically computed by your tool.

	BP	SP	BP/SP
E3	23.30	3	7.77
E7	28.25	5	5.65
E2	45.13	8	5.64
E4	17.31	5	3.46
E8	26.66	8	3.33
E1	24.80	8	3.10
E5	30.09	13	2.31
E6	15.45	13	1.19
Total	211	63	3.35

	Benefit	Cost	Benefit/Cost
E3	8.45	1.80	4.69
E7	10.24	3.00	3.41
E2	16.36	4.80	3.41
E4	6.28	3.00	2.09
E8	9.67	4.80	2.01
E1	8.99	4.80	1.87
E5	10.91	7.80	1.40
E6	5.60	7.80	0.72
Total	76.50	37.80	2.02

Fig. 3.16 Left: Benefit-cost index (BP/SP), with effect benefit points (BP) divided by size points (SP), sorted in descending order. Right: Benefit/cost, where the points are instantiated at 1 BP = 0.36 million and 1 SP = 0.6 million, sorted in descending order.

when providing estimates, by using, for example, size points and benefit points. Several existing methods do not explicitly support separating these concerns. The result is, again, a confounding of concepts, with ensuing confusion as to how to proceed with benefit-cost deliberations.

We introduced our approach to over 500 IT professionals in a triannual industry workshop on agile management. When participants first inadvertently attempted to estimate benefit without a clear picture of the objectives and returns, they expressed frustration over having to keep track of large numbers of factors at the same time. After being encouraged to concentrate on one relation at a time, they found that complexity disappeared and perceived the task as easy.

Jumbled concepts and a lack of clarity regarding the estimation task one is currently undertaking are not unusual. We regularly witness, in projects and larger development programmes, how notions akin to objectives, returns, and various metrics are confounded. This seems to create a dull confusion, halting effective benefits management. Although you might want to use other notions for goals than the objectives and returns in this book, we encourage you to adopt a disciplined approach to those notions and to be deliberate about exactly what you are estimating at a given time.

Although relatively new, the concepts presented in this paper have started to emerge in various organizations. Several projects in the public and private sectors have used benefit points to estimate the contribution of epics to business objectives, and subsequently used this for backlog prioritization. MISHRI has turned out to be a particularly popular technique, since it has made it possible for project leaders to include soft returns when presenting business cases for senior management and prioritizing backlogs. The general feedback from project members so far is that the benefit estimation process yields improvements over earlier practice, particularly in terms of a better understanding of project objectives and a clearer perception of the expected value of project deliverables. Benefit estimation also contributes to aligning project and business resources with respect to the impacts to expect from project deliverables.

Throughout this discussion, those portions of tables that you are required to provide estimates for have white backgrounds. Portions that are automatically calculated by your tool (e.g. Excel), have shaded backgrounds. Note that a modest number of expert estimates need to be provided and that they are not complicated measures, but are intended to capture the project's knowledge that is currently available.

The remainder of this chapter contains optional sections, which can be skipped in a first reading and consulted if needed. They contain material that addresses more frequent questions people have asked us when teaching or using these techniques. For example, see Section 3.19 for comparisons with other, related techniques, and Section 3.20 for more on the underlying principles of our techniques.

3.15*   Benefit Poker

The key to assigning benefit points is to assess how much you think each epic contributes to the project's objectives. Here, we describe how to adapt the familiar practice of planning poker to a game of benefit poker. We illustrate this with effect points.

A benefit poker session could proceed as follows. A group of stakeholders estimates the relative contributions to an objective, one epic at a time. Each stakeholder bids a number face down, after which everyone reveals their bid simultaneously. The stakeholders with the highest and lowest bids are prompted to express their grounds for their bids. In this way, different assumptions and perspectives on the product element (and the objective) are highlighted. Nuances in understanding, knowledge, experiences, and ambitions contribute to useful clarifications and refinements. A host of group processes will likely be ongoing in such sessions, perhaps not all of them beneficial, but the rationale is that the positive effects of such poker sessions still outweigh the negative.

Bid rounds continue until the bids converge towards common agreement. In our experience, three rounds often suffices. If the bids still deviate substantially, the product owner can choose the average bid or the majority (if six of eight have identical bids, say). The resulting number represents the benefit points for the epic on the given objective. The group then turns to the next epic in the backlog and estimates its relative contribution to the same objective as before by repeating the bidding procedure.

It is common in planning poker to use a standard card deck with a slightly revised Fibonacci sequence, namely, 0, 1/2, 1, 2, 3, 5, 8, 13, 20, 40, 100 [4]. Grenning's [15] original paper on planning poker used a set of cards with the sequence 1, 2, 3, 5, 7, 10, ∞. The author also stated that the participants should feel free to use sums by showing two cards at once. This is also a practice we have used successfully. The important thing is not the Fibonacci numbers as such, but that the values are on a ratio scale and that the scale enables good differentiation between estimates.

Benefit poker can be used for both *parts of the whole* assessment (percentages, distributing 100 points, etc.; see Section 3.3) and open-ended scales (Section 3.12). The Fibonacci sequence can be used in both cases. To distribute 100 points, say, use the deck of cards above, with 100 as the highest number. To distribute 100 linear points, use cards from zero to 100, perhaps in intervals of one, five, or 10.

The argument for using the Fibonacci sequence would be to adapt the state of practice in cost estimation to benefit estimation. There is, however, no evidence yet to determine which scale provides better accuracy and reliability in assessments. It has been argued that the Fibonacci sequence is favourable due to what is known as the *Weber-Fechner* law [8]: as magnitudes increase, it becomes harder to distinguish between them. In fact, differences between magnitudes must increase exponentially for our senses to be able to detect the differences. Use of the Fibonacci sequence would then facilitate differentiation.

On the other hand, one study [46] suggests that the use of the Fibonacci sequence leads to lower estimates, on average, than the use of a uniformly distributed scale (e.g. 1, 2, 3, 4, 5, 6, ...), possibly due to the *central tendency of judgement* effect [24], where assessors tend towards the middle value of the perceived pool of possible values. In a standard deck of Fibonacci-style planning poker cards, as above, the middle value is five; that is, substantially lower than the middle value of a zero–100 linear scale. In cost estimation, where the general tendency is to give estimates that are too low, this can exacerbate the situation. In benefit estimation, it is not yet known if, or in what direction, estimates tend to deviate from actual values. If the general trait is overoptimism, one would expect benefit estimates to tend to be too high. However, even if the Fibonacci sequence can counter this tendency, its use for that purpose would ostensibly be for the wrong reason if due to the effect above.

3.16* One Combined Objective

Assessing epics against a number of objectives can seem quite complex. In practice, effect point estimation can be quite rapid. The stakeholder team will likely need a few moments to get calibrated to the scale it is using (perhaps starting with a reference epic), but once at cruising altitude, our experience is that it takes only a couple of hours to assess 10 to 20 epics on four to six objectives.

However, an alternative to considering several objectives is to estimate the effects of epics on some notion of a single objective. This practice is common today, where, for example, issuing one or several pluses (+) or minuses (-) to pieces of functionality against some potentially unspecified notion of benefit is a prevalent mode of operation.

Ostensibly, there are pros and cons to both approaches. The consideration of specific objectives allows one to think in more detail, but substantially increases the complexity of the benefit point estimation process. On the other hand, considering all objectives as one single, perhaps fuzzy entity can mean that you, as a stakeholder, are not really able to use your expertise and knowledge of the domain properly, even though the estimation process is substantially less complex.

There are theoretical grounds for choosing the first, more complex approach. Judgement and decision making theories predict that people will be affected by a host of unconscious biases that are likely to affect judgement in ways that can neither be predicted nor controlled [30, 17]. These biases add considerable noise to judgements. However, if one is able to use *task-specific* knowledge at key points in the judgement process, one should be able to boost the conscious elements in the judgement process, so that the decisions are the results of knowledge to a greater extent [38]. This is a case for strengthening the signal of a conscious knowledge-based process over the noise of unconscious biases. Consideration of each objective in turn stimulates that conscious signal.

Empirically, a controlled experiment indicates that the first approach generates estimates with less inter-rater variance than the second approach. This phenomenon could be a manifestation of lower noise, as theorized above. Additionally, less variance between job performers is an indication that a task has been defined such that expertise both is applicable and can be built [31, 7].

3.17* Life Cycle Cost Estimation

In Section 2.4, we stated that, to obtain a sensible expression of benefit/cost, the estimates of cost must take into account the life cycle of the product element, not only its construction. Size points (Section 3.8) reflect life cycle costs, and a simplifying assumption is that life cycle costs can be computed as proportions of the estimated *build cost*. In this section, we provide simple heuristics for doing so.

Here, we define the estimated build cost b as the estimated cost of development and unit testing of a specific product element. Thus, b is typically a value that can be verified after sprints and the basis of sprint burndown charts. Then, to arrive at an estimated *construction cost* for the product element, we need to add hours necessary for design, integration testing, documentation, and ceremonies, which will depend on the organization's development methods and standards. Experience from several large public sector organizations suggests that this sum ends up in the neighbourhood of $2b$.

To arrive at a *release cost* estimate for the product element, work related to product ownership, architecture, management, and operations must also be accounted for. This will again depend on how development is organized in the enterprise. Experience tells us that this release cost can amount to somewhere around $6b$. This is also called the *investment cost* of the product element, which can be verified at the end of a release.

To arrive at a *life cycle cost* estimate, we must now take into account two more cost drivers:

- Work related to teaching and motivating the end users and other stakeholders and
- Work related to maintenance (bug fixes, simple changes, and software component upgrades) after the first deployment.

The cost of these drivers can be estimated as proportions of the investment cost. Again, these proportions depend on the methodology and the organization. Let i be the investment cost. In one public agency, the first driver above turns out to be, on average, approximately $0.15i$, while the second driver is stipulated to vary over four years in production, as follows: $0.15i$ for the first year and $0.12i$, $0.11i$, and $0.10i$ for the following years. Using these rules of thumb yields a life cycle cost over four years of $9.78b$. For other public agencies, the factors are similar to these, but not identical.

The exact factors by which to multiply the build cost will vary according to the type of project, and the above factors should be considered merely as examples. The take away is that the life cycle cost can be estimated as proportional to the build cost.

Of course, there will be uncertainty in all of this. However, although the life cycle cost estimate as a whole will have a slow evaluation cycle, one can adjust the factors involved after sprints and releases according to incremental experience, thus removing some of the uncertainty.

Hardware and other infrastructure cost drivers might have to be computed separately. For example, one might distribute these cost elements at either the project level or the enterprise portfolio level down to the product elements in question.

The main thing to bear in mind is that the life cycle cost estimates should be computed for the same time period as the benefit estimates. We return to periodization and the concept of present value in Chapter 7.

3.18* Negative Benefit

Product elements can have a negative effect on objectives. Consider again our example project in Fig. 3.2, where *Obj1* is 'Reduce average case processing time by 30%'. Suppose the stakeholders and product owner want to include the following new epic *E9* in the backlog: 'As a security officer in the agency, I want to perform a check of the applicant for a certificate of good conduct before granting the application'. The epic might not be that costly, but it will impact the average case processing time in a negative manner. The project can consider other epics to compensate for this negative impact, so that *Obj1* will still be met.

Objectives can also add negative worth to returns. Consider again the example project in Fig. 3.2, where we now introduce *Obj4*, 'Case processing should fully meet the new quality and security standards'. Objectives such as this can be costly and, moreover, conflict with other objectives and impact returns in a negative manner. For our specific example project, the stakeholders could decide that, to meet this objective, the agency will have to allocate resources to the relevant departments, and they could estimate that *Obj4* will have a negative impact on *Ret1* ('Reduced number of man-hours').

Since benefit points are purely relative estimates, negative benefit can be handled by assigning monetary benefit point values so that benefit points below a certain threshold represent a negative monetary value. For example, if using a 100-point scale, one could set the zero point at 50 benefit points and set 1 benefit point at 3.7 million for all amounts of benefit points above 50, and 1 benefit point at -3.7

million for all amounts of benefit points below 50. However, this can be awkward, especially if using the Fibonacci scale, since the distances between negative values will always be smaller than the distances between positive values.

A better alternative is to use explicit positive and negative benefit points. Consider the benefit points from the Fibonacci sequence in Fig. 3.12. The effect points for the new epic *E9* above could be estimated at -8 on *Obj1* (contrasting the positive impact of epic *E4* on the same objective), zero for *Obj2* (no impact on 'number of wrong case decisions'), and -5 for *Obj3* (contrasting the positive impact for *E2* on *Obj3*).

3.19*   Other Approaches

Agile at scale frameworks, such as Large Scale Scrum (LeSS) and Scaled Agile Framework (SAFe) present alternative models for prioritizing product elements, or product backlog items, as they are referred to in these frameworks. In LeSS, one is prompted to, 'with *relative value points* (RVPs) as a lightweight proxy for "value", use *planning poker* to experiment with *relative value points* (RVPs) and their estimation' [34, p. 139]. This method is not described in detail. Instead, it is argued that value is not a simple attribute or number, and one is advised to move beyond the simplistic notion of value towards multiple weighted factors, such as stakeholder preferences, strategic alignment, relative points for value and effort, and risk.

In SAFe, the prioritization of product backlog items is based on several parameters. Building on the concept of the *cost of delay* [39], one should use an algorithm to compute the sequence to implement the product backlog items [35]. This approach is called the *weighted shortest job first* (WSJF) method:

$$\text{WSJF} = (\text{User-Business Value} + \text{Time Criticality} + \text{Risk Reduction \& Opportunity Enablement Value})/\text{Job Size}$$

where the indicated parameters are estimated with relative sizes using the Fibonacci sequence. The complexity of these measures contrasts with what we are advocating. Combining benefit, cost, risk, and duration parameters in one go is not easy and mixing different parameters can inhibit measuring, reporting, and project learning.

We designed the current framework to be intuitive and straightforward to maintain, and the key to this is the clear separation between the cost and benefit parameters. Our approach is minted towards supporting stakeholders' conscious processes.

3.20*   Satisficing, Fast, and Frugal

Human-based benefit and cost estimation are judgement-based tasks. Such tasks are often inherently difficult and *inconsistent* (with different people developing different successful strategies) [1, 3, 2] and *ill structured* (where it is hard to even define successful strategies) [26, 43, 40, 48]. Research shows that practitioners of inconsistent and ill-structured tasks can apparently spend their careers *not* learning and *not* improving their performance beyond a very narrow subset of consistent tasks [28, 42].

In the field of judgement and decision making, cognition is often modelled as two sets of subprocesses: the *analytical* and the *intuitive*. The former is deliberate and strives to take into account all relevant cues. It is therefore slow. The latter relies on only a few cues, might not be fully conscious, and is regarded as rapid.

There are reasons to favour the analytical process; after all, rational thinking, taking into consideration all relevant factors with a tight focus on explicit deliberation [41], adds comprehensiveness [9] and is something most of us are trained to value (e.g. the so-called *worship of reason* [16]). Several studies show how humans ostensibly fail to make correct judgements when they do not follow analytical processes, due to biases and undue heuristics [29, 47].

However, human working memory and other cognitive functions limit humans' ability to process all relevant factors, let alone rapidly, when the number of factors becomes large and the relations complex [37, 13]. A large body of research has investigated how to take advantage of the quicker intuitive processes, including the fast and frugal heuristics approach to judgement and decision making [13, 19, 20, 12] and naturalistic decision making [32, 36, 18]. All of these approaches acknowledge the almost impossible task of supplying the sufficiently reliable information required to predict accurately how to proceed in complex situations. Both human decision makers and tools fail to deliver good results under uncertain circumstances when attempting to gather and analyse all relevant data correctly. Instead, it is argued, human cognitive judgement is geared towards processing unreliable partial information rapidly and with sufficient accuracy for the purpose at hand, in line with *satisficing*, rather than optimizing [44]. Following this argumentation, we determine that methods and tools should be designed to support this mode of decision making, rather than geared towards analysing the totality of a situation [13].

The underlying principles in our methods are in line with these ideas. We design our methods so that stakeholders

- Consider a limited number of cues at a time and a single relation at a time,
- Provide a modest number of assessments (the white portions of the tables in this book), from which additional measures are automatically calculated in a transparent manner (the shaded portions of the tables), and
- Perform relative points-based estimations by comparing product elements, rather than producing absolute monetary estimates on individual product elements.

Moreover, the methods are designed to facilitate project and community learning. In Hogarth's [22, 21] terms, intuition is expertise that is internalized [6], perhaps after extended experience and deliberate practice [7]. Intuition can therefore be trained. Klein [32] suggests aiming to learn like an expert, that is, provide meth-

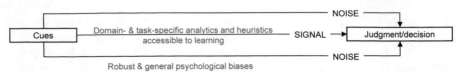

Fig. 3.17 Processes amenable to learning (signal) and processes robust to learning (noise).

ods and tools that support *learning to become* an expert, in addition to *acting* as an expert. Accordingly [32, 33], we design our methods so that stakeholders

- Engage in *deliberate practice* by assessing and reassessing product elements that are associated with goals (returns) and evaluation criteria (objectives),
- Obtain *feedback that is accurate and diagnostic and reasonably timely* by evaluating and re-evaluating assigned benefit points and size points and their monetary values, following stakeholders' evaluation of MVPs in increments, and
- Enrich *experiences by reviewing prior experiences to derive new insights and lessons from mistakes* by using points-based estimates to monitor project progress.

The facility to access relevant domain knowledge systematically is central to learning. For inconsistent tasks, it is important to stimulate processes that are sensitive to domain knowledge [38, 32] and learning [7]. These processes can be seen to increase the desired signal against the noise of competing processes that are driven by general psychological traits that are not domain specific and not amenable to learning [30, 11, 19, 20, 23, 12] (see Fig. 3.17). In the spirit of Stewart [45], one must increase the reliability of estimates, in the sense of decreasing undue inter- and intra-rater variance. We do want variance in a group of diverse stakeholders due to their respective domain- and task-relevant perspectives, but we do not want variance due to the misperceptions or inaccessibility of the knowledge in question and the host of undue biases. We advocate methods such as relative and pairwise comparisons that help stakeholders tap into domain knowledge and structure its use in assessments. Pairwise comparisons are a core element in the conscious cognitive processes of judgement[38]. To strengthen conscious comparisons further, methods that focus on differences are beneficial (e.g. the repertory grid technique [10]). We also advocate structured group methods that are intended to elicit and illuminate domain knowledge from various perspectives.

References

1. P.L. Ackerman, "Individual differences in skill learning: An integration of psychometric and information processing perspectives," *Psychological Bulletin*, vol. 102, pp. 3–27, 1987.
2. J.P. Campbell, "Modeling the performance prediction problem in industrial and organizational psychology," in *Handbook of Industrial and Organizational Psychology*, M.D. Dunnette and L.M. Hough, Eds. Consulting Psychologists Press, Inc., 1990, vol. 1, pp. 687–732.
3. J.P. Campbell, R.A. McCloy, S.H. Oppler, and C.E. Sager, "A theory of performance," in *Personnel Selection in Organizations*, N. Schmitt and W.C. Borman, Eds. Josey-Bass, 1993, pp. 35–70.
4. M. Cohn, *Agile Estimating and Planning*. Prentice Hall, 2005.
5. M. Denne and J. Cleland-Huang, *Software by Numbers: Low-Risk, High-Return Development*. Prentice Hall, 2003.

6. H.L. Dreyfus and S.E. Dreyfus, *Mind over Machine*. The Free Press, 1988.
7. K.A. Ericsson, "An introduction to Cambridge Handbook of Expertise and Expert Performance: Its development, organization, and content," in *The Cambridge Handbook of Expertise and Expert Performance*, K.A. Ericsson, N. Charness, P.J. Feltovich, and R.R. Hoffman, Eds. Cambridge Univ. Press, 2006, ch. 1, pp. 3–20.
8. G.T. Fechner, *Elemente der Psychophysik – Erster Teil*. Breitkopf und Härtel, 1860.
9. D.P. Forbes, "Reconsidering the strategic implications of decision comprehensiveness," *Academy of Management Review*, vol. 32, no. 2, pp. 361–376, 2007.
10. F. Fransella, R. Bell, and D. Bannister, *A Manual for Repertory Grid Technique*. John Wiley & Sons, Ltd., 2004.
11. G. Gigerenzer, *Gut Feelings. The Intelligence of the Unconscious*. Viking, Penguin, Ltd., 2007.
12. G. Gigerenzer and D.G. Goldstein, "Reasoning the fast and frugal way: Models of bounded rationality," *Psychological Review*, vol. 103, no. 4, pp. 650–669, 1996.
13. G. Gigerenzer and P.M. Todd, Eds., *Simple Heuristics that Make Us Smart*. Oxford University Press, 1999.
14. T. Gilb, *Competitive Engineering—A Handbook For Systems Engineering, Requirements Engineering, and Software Engineering Using Planguage*. Butterworth-Heinemann, 2005.
15. J.W. Grenning, "Planning poker or how to avoid analysis paralysis while release planning," 2002.
16. J. Haidt, "The emotional dog and its rational tail: A social intuitionist approach to moral judgment," *Psychological Review*, vol. 108, pp. 814–834, 2001.
17. T. Halkjelsvik and M. Jørgensen, "From origami to software development: A review of studies on judgment-based predictions of performance time," *accepted to Psychological Bulletin*, 2012.
18. K.R. Hammond, "Upon reflection," *Thinking and Reasoning*, vol. 2, no. 2/3, pp. 239–248, 1996.
19. R. Hertwig, U. Hoffrage, and L. Martignon, "Quick estimation: Letting the environment do the work," in *Simple Heuristics that Make Us Smart*, G. Gigerenzer and P.M. Todd, Eds. Oxford University Press, 1999, ch. 10, pp. 75–95.
20. U. Hoffrage, R. Hertwig, and G. Gigerenzer, "Hindsight bias: a by-product of knowledge updating?" *Journal of Experimental Psychology: Learning, Memory and Cognition*, vol. 26, pp. 566–581, 2000.
21. R. Hogarth, "Beyond discrete biases: Functional and dysfunctional aspects of judgmental heuristics," *Psychological Bulletin*, vol. 90, no. 2, pp. 197–217, 1981.
22. R.M. Hogarth, *Educating Intuition*. The University of Chicago Press, 2001.
23. R.M. Hogarth, "When simple is hard to accept," in *Ecological Rationality: Intelligence in the World*, P.M. Todd and G. Gigerenzer, Eds. Oxford University Press, 2006.
24. H.L. Hollingworth, "A survey of the characteristics of projects with success in delivering client benefits," *The Journal of Philosophy, Psychology and Scientific Methods*, vol. 7, no. 17, pp. 461–469, 1910.
25. International Institute of Business Analysis, "A guide to the business analysis body of knowledge," 2009.
26. E.J. Johnson, "Expertise and decision under uncertainty: Performance and process," in *The Nature of Expertise*, M.T.H. Chi, R. Glaser, and M.J. Farr, Eds. Lawrence Erlbaum Associates, Inc., 1988, pp. 209–228.
27. C. Jones, *Estimating Software Costs: Bringing Realism to Estimating*, 2nd ed. McGraw-Hill, 2007.
28. M. Jørgensen, "Forecasting of software development work effort: Evidence on expert judgement and formal models," *Int'l J. Forecasting*, vol. 23, pp. 449–462, 2007.
29. D. Kahneman and S. Frederick, "A model of heuristic judgment," in *The Cambridge Handbook of Thinking and Reasoning*, K.J. Holyoak and R.G. Morrison, Eds. Cambridge Univ. Press, 2004, pp. 267–294.
30. D. Kahneman and G. Klein, "Conditions for intuitive expertise—a failure to disagree," *American Psychologist*, vol. 64, no. 6, pp. 515–526, 2009.

31. C.T. Keil and J.M. Cortina, "Degradation of validity over time: A test and extension of acker-man's model," *Psychological Bulletin*, vol. 127, pp. 673–697, 1987.
32. G. Klein, "Developing expertise in decision making," *Thinking & Reasoning*, vol. 3, no. 4, pp. 337–352, 1997.
33. G. Klein, *Sources of Power: How People Make Decisions.* MIT Press, 1998.
34. C. Larman and B. Vodde, *Practices for Scaling Lean & Agile Development: Large, Multisite, and Offshore Product Development with Large-Scale Scrum.* Addison Wesley, 2010.
35. D. Leffingwell, *Agile Software Requirements: Lean Requirements Practices for Teams, Programs and the Enterprise.* Addison Wesley, 2011.
36. R. Lipshitz, G. Klein, J. Orasanu, and E. Salas, "Rejoinder: A welcome dialogue – and the need to continue," *J. Behavioral Decision Making*, pp. 385–389, 2001.
37. G.A. Miller, "The magical number seven, plus or minus two: Some limits on our capacity for processing information," *Psychological Review*, vol. 63, pp. 81–97, 1956.
38. T. Mussweiler, "Comparison processes in social judgment: Mechanisms and consequences," *Psych. Review*, vol. 110, no. 3, pp. 472–489, 2003.
39. D. Reinertsen, *Principles of Product Development Flow: Second Generation Lean Product Development.* Celeritas Publishing, 2009.
40. W. Reitman, *Cognition and Thought.* Wiley, 1965.
41. E. Salas, M.A. Rosen, and D. DiazGranados, "Expertise-based intuition and decision making in organizations," *Journal of Management*, vol. 36, no. 4, pp. 941–973, 2010.
42. J. Shanteau, "Competence in experts: The role of task characteristics," *Organizational Behavior and Human Decision Processes*, vol. 53, pp. 252–266, 1992.
43. H.A. Simon, "The structure of ill-structured problems," *Artificial Intelligence*, vol. 4, pp. 181–201, 1973.
44. H.A. Simon, *The Sciences of the Artificial*, 3rd ed. MIT Press, 1996.
45. T.R. Stewart, "Improving reliability of judgmental forecasts," in *Principles of Forecasting: A Handbook for Researchers and Practitioners*, J.S. Armstrong, Ed. Kluwer Academic Publishers, 2001, pp. 81–106.
46. R. Tamrakar and M. Jørgenseni, "Does the use of Fibonacci numbers in planning poker affect effort estimates," in *Proc. 16th International Conference on Evaluation & Assessment in Software Engineering (EASE 2012)*, 2012, pp. 228–232.
47. A. Tversky and D. Kahneman, "Judgement under uncertainty: Heuristics and biases," *Science*, vol. 185, no. 27, pp. 1124–1131, Sept. 1974.
48. J.F. Voss and T.A. Post, "On the solving of ill-structured problems," in *The Nature of Expertise*, M.T.H. Chi, R. Glaser, and M.J. Farr, Eds. Lawrence Erlbaum Associates, Inc., 1988, pp. 261–285.

Chapter 4
Benefit Points for the Portfolio

> Business is often about killing
> your favourite children to allow
> others to succeed.
>
> JOHN HARVEY-JONES

Abstract The methodological principles for assigning benefit points to product elements within a project can also be used at the portfolio level. This allows for the management of entire portfolios towards optimizing benefit over cost. We consider bottom-up assessments from the projects at the portfolio level and top-down assessments at the portfolio level within projects. We revisit the confirmatory and exploratory modes.

4.1 Overview

Many organizations run not one project at a time, but several. Often, they will have some sort of notion of portfolio to encompass these projects and a form of portfolio management that exerts varying degrees of coordination over the projects. In many cases, this amounts almost exclusively to cost control.

However, portfolios provide explicit opportunities to take advantage of the type of benefits management that we address in this book. When a project finds that the benefit-cost ratio in its backlog is no longer opportune, resources can be transferred from that project elsewhere within the portfolio. A portfolio is the framework within which cost and resources can be distributed so that benefit can be optimized across several projects to reach the organization's overall goals.

Although common sense and obviously a good idea, thinking and acting along these lines is sometimes surprisingly hard. One of several reasons is that more or less autonomous projects compete for funding and resources, even within the same organization. There is then limited willingness among project managers to give up their allotted funding and resources, whatever the good reasons from a wider perspective.

Portfolio management is a complex theme. The contribution of this chapter is that benefit points provide a visible metric that makes it possible to discuss the viability of continuing a project to the bitter end. We also suggest how benefit points can be

J. E. Hannay, *Benefit/Cost-Driven Agile Software Development*,
Simula SpringerBriefs on Computing 8,
https://doi.org/10.1007/978-3-030-74218-8_4

used explicitly in a portfolio-wide manner to support portfolio-wide decisions about
benefit/cost.

We first illustrate how the points-based benefit and cost estimates for individual
projects can be combined into portfolio estimates. This approach builds portfolio
estimates from the project up. We then illustrate how one can provide estimates
directly at the portfolio level. This approach allows us to derive project estimates
from the portfolio in a top-down manner.

4.2 Portfolio Composition

The projects methods covered in the previous chapter can be applied at the portfolio
level. Figure 4.1 shows the project (Fig. 3.1) in a portfolio perspective schematically
as part of the agile fractal (Fig.2.6). Several projects contribute to common portfolio
goals. Whereas a purely project-oriented view, as in the previous chapter, can be
myopically ignorant of surrounding projects and wider goals, the portfolio view
requires that projects relate to common goals.

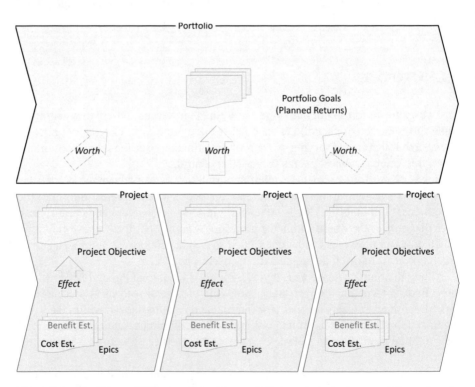

Fig. 4.1 A schematic portfolio of projects. The portfolio has planned returns, and the project objectives are planned to fulfil the portfolio returns.

	Ret1	Ret2	Ret3		Weight	
millions:	100	40	60	Total	Project	Enterprise
Project A						
Obj1	...	...	...	...	...	...
...	...	...	...	...	...	...
ObjN$_A$	...	...	...	...	...	...
Total A	0.10	0.55	0.40	56.00	1.00	0.28
Project B						
Obj1	0.10	0.10	0.125	21.50	0.28	0.11
Obj2	0.10	0.15	0.15	25.00	0.33	0.13
Obj3	0.20	0.10	0.10	30.00	0.39	0.15
Total B	0.40	0.35	0.375	76.50	1.00	0.38
Project C						
Obj1	...	...	...	...	...	...
...	...	...	...	...	...	...
ObjN$_C$	...	...	...	...	...	...
Total C	0.50	0.10	0.225	67.50	1	0.34
Total Portfolio	1	1	1	200.00		1

Fig. 4.2 The objectives' contribution to returns for an example project in a portfolio in terms of worth benefit points. The returns are given monetary value (in millions of your favourite currency). One obtains the results in the 'Total' column, to the right of the 'Return' columns, by multiplying those goals by each objective's expected contributions and summing the results. For example, for Project B's *Obj1*, (100 * 0.10) + (40 * 0.10) + (60 * 0.125) = 21.50. Compare this to Figs. 3.4 and 3.5.

Figure 4.2 shows the example project from the previous chapter (now project *B*) from this perspective. Here, worth points are given as proportions of the objectives' worth on returns. This is the confirmatory mode, where proportions are used rather than 'parts of 100', for variation. For example, project *B*'s *Obj1* is assessed as contributing 10% of the portfolio's total return on *Ret1*, and *Ret1* is set at half the total planned return of the portfolio (concretized with 100 million in your favourite currency). The 'Sum' column presents the resulting total estimated worth of each objective, and the 'Weight' columns present the objectives' corresponding relative weights, with respect to the project and to the portfolio, respectively. You should verify that this is consistent with Figs. 3.4 and 3.5.

These assessments allow the portfolio management group to contemplate the combined objectives of the portfolio's projects. Combining the total project benefit and cost estimates provides a benefit-cost index at the portfolio level. Figure 4.3 exemplifies this for our example project *B* with the two other projects in the portfolio. Here, one should take into consideration the fact that project *A* has the highest estimated benefit/cost value.

There are various ways to use this type of information. One could contemplate initiating this project first, or allocating more resources to it and perhaps to the next best one (project *B*). One could wait to make any such decisions until completing sensitivity analyses on waste elimination. For example, how is benefit/cost affected by dropping *E6* from project *B* and similar unfortunate epics from the other projects?

Moreover, in a given project, one can stop construction when the benefit/cost is no longer defendable and reallocate resources to another project in the portfolio whose queue does have benefit/cost-viable product elements.

Other factors also determine the actual sequence in which product elements are put into construction, especially in portfolio management. The final cut is made during portfolio release planning, which is described extensively in literature elsewhere.

The presence of a benefit-cost index in portfolio management can counteract the tendency for individual projects to stovepipe themselves and compete with each other. The index explicitly implies that giving up resources for the success of the portfolio, and therefore the organization, can make sense.

Project	Benefit	Cost	Benefit/Cost
A	56.00	13.40	4.18
B	76.50	37.80	2.02
C	67.50	36.20	1.86
Total	200.00	87.40	2.29

Fig. 4.3 Project benefit-cost index for use at the portfolio level.

Case 6. A federal organization in charge of procuring and developing systems for the defence sector routinely initiates and runs a large number (hundreds) of concurrent projects, several of which are budgeted in the hundreds of millions of US dollars. Traditionally, projects compete with each other for resources, and the task of managing this bundle of projects in an optimal manner is perceived to be extremely challenging. This has resulted in the suboptimal interoperability of systems, inadvertent duplications of functionality across systems, undeployed functionality, and other unfortunate consequences. However, the body responsible for administering the mandatory procurement and development process model has stated that, since projects are run according to the initial ratified plan, with the aim of spending their entire budget, benefits management during the course of a project would not be helpful.

Awareness of such cases as the one above has been raised, and information technology governance bodies in several countries are placing more emphasis on benefits management during development in their IT strategies and roadmaps. Benefit point estimation techniques constitute a tool set designed to help practitioners to perform benefits management actively during development.

4.3 Worth Points in the Exploratory Mode

In Section 3.12, we explained how to use open-ended scales, such as the Fibonacci numbers, for effect points. One can also use open-ended scales for worth points. Figure 4.4 shows an assessment of objectives' contributions to returns using Fibonacci numbers, for a total of 104 worth points for the portfolio.

Again, open-ended scales can result in unequal benefit point totals on the criteria. Here, the return totals (35, 33, 36) are slightly different. As for effect points, differences in worth point totals can be (A) an artefact of the estimation method or (B) an assessment that the returns are fulfilled to different degrees. For (A), see Section 4.5. Here we look at (B), that is, worth points in the exploratory mode. We do so analogously to the discussion for effect points in Sections 3.12.

4.3.1 Exploring the Worth of Objectives

The differences in worth point totals per return could indicate that the stakeholder group does not consider the projects' objectives to be worth what is stipulated in the returns. This would prompt discussions to re-evaluate the project objectives (which could, in turn, uncover a need to re-evaluate the projects' epics).

	Ret1	Ret2	Ret3	Total
Project A				
$Obj1_A$	...	...	...	...
...	...	...	...	...
$ObjN_A$	...	...	...	...
Total A	6	18	11	35
Project B				
$Obj1_B$	3	3	5	11
$Obj2_B$	3	5	5	13
$Obj3_B$	5	1	8	14
Total B	11	9	18	38
Project C				
$Obj3_C$	...	...	...	...
...	...	...	...	...
$ObjN_C$	...	...	...	...
Total C	18	6	7	31
Total Portfolio	35	33	36	104

Fig. 4.4 A portfolio of three projects with relative estimates (worth benefit points) in terms of Fibonacci numbers.

4.3.2   Exploring the Feasibility of Returns

The differences in worth point totals per return can also indicate that the portfolio returns are not appropriate. Stakeholders at the strategic levels would then re-evaluate the portfolio's planned returns.

In a more deliberate fashion, stakeholders can use the exploratory mode actively to fix the value of returns. For example, they would know that the organization or customer wants to reduce man-hours, but would have to explore the extent to which the portfolio under development is capable of doing so, and thus what monetary value the 'reduce number of man-hours' return holds. Such deliberations then set the monetary value of the effect points used in Section 3.10.

(The astute reader might ask why we are not setting the monetary value of worth points. If you are interested in this question, see Section 4.6.)

4.4   Portfolio Decomposition

The agile fractal (Fig. 2.6) shows how the concept of product elements is applicable at several levels and to other units of functionality besides epics. In a portfolio, it is possible to view entire projects as product elements in the form of super epics. Figure 4.5 shows how super epics that represent entire projects are assessed directly on returns.

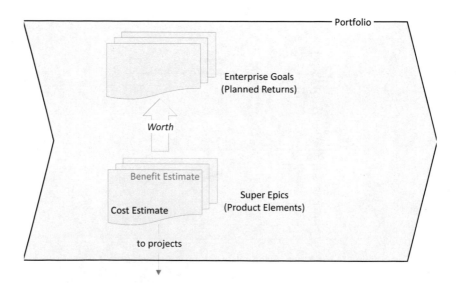

Fig. 4.5 Super epics for projects as product elements, with portfolio returns as benefit criteria.

	Ret1	Ret2	Ret3	Total
Super Epic A	0.10	0.55	0.40	1
Super Epic B	0.40	0.35	0.375	1
Super Epic C	0.50	0.10	0.225	1
Total Portfolio	1	1	1	3

Fig. 4.6 Assessment of super epics for entire projects on returns, confirmatory mode.

At this stage, super epics are incepted at the portfolio level and given overall benefit and cost estimates, prior to distribution at the project level.

This view of projects as product elements is very abstract. It does not consider any project objectives. It is particularly suited to the very early stages in a portfolio's inception, perhaps to obtain an initial overview of the portfolio's projects. This can be accomplished in both the confirmatory and exploratory modes.

Figure 4.6 illustrates the three projects in our example portfolio, assessed as super epics in their contribution to portfolio returns. This illustrates the confirmatory mode and corresponds to Fig. 4.2, but, here, the stakeholder group has not included any project objectives in their assessments. They are assuming that the portfolio returns are to be fulfilled as such and are assessing what proportion of each return the projects will fulfil.

In the exploratory mode using Fibonacci numbers, the assessment could look like Fig. 4.7. Here, the stakeholder group could be exploring the power of the projects

	Ret1	Ret2	Ret3	Total
Super Epic A	1	13	3	17
Super Epic B	3	3	8	14
Super Epic C	5	1	2	8
Total Portfolio	9	17	13	39

Fig. 4.7 Assessment of super epics for entire projects on returns, exploratory mode.

to fulfil the returns, or they could be determining how to quantify the returns (which could be rudimentarily declared at this stage).

Case 7. A public service enterprise that administers loans conducted benefit assessments of five projects within a portfolio on six strategic goals (returns), as shown in the following table.

Project	Customer Satisfaction	Processing Time	Digital Dialogue	Productivity	Leaning & Culture	Expert Body	Total
Internal Collaboration	13	4	9	25	28	18	97
New Application Process	20	17	17	40	5	7	106
Extended Support Period	40	0.5	0	6	5	0.6	52
Digital Signature	14	0	15	5	3	7	44
Continuous Improvement	4	3	3	13	2	2	27
Total	91	24.5	44	89	43	35	326
Degree of fulfilment	0.91	0.25	0.44	0.89	0.43	0.35	

The stakeholder group used planning poker cards with a variant of the Fibonacci sequence (0, 0.5, 1, 2, 3, 5, 8, 13, 20, 40, 100). Disputes were sometimes resolved by averaging the poker bids, resulting in non-Fibonacci values in the table above. Noticeably, the sequence was not used as an open-ended scale. Instead it was decided that the numbers should signify degrees of the fulfilment of returns, with 100 denoting total fulfilment. Thus, the group employed the partial fulfilment of objectives (see Section 3.12.4).

Returns in the capacity of objectives were weighted directly using the model for integrating soft and hard returns on investment (or MISHRI; see Section 3.11), as shown in the following table.

Project weight:	Customer Satisfaction 75	Processing Time 75	Digital Dialogue 50	Productivity 100	Leaning & Culture 25	Expert Body 75	Total
Internal Collaboration	9.8	3.0	4.5	25.0	7.0	13.5	62.8
New Application Process	15.0	12.8	8.5	40.0	1.3	5.3	82.8
Extended Support Period	30.0	0.4	0.0	6.0	1.3	0.5	38.1
Digital Signature	10.5	0.0	7.5	5.0	0.8	5.3	29.0
Continuous Improvement	3.0	2.3	1.5	13.0	0.5	1.5	21.8
Total	68.3	18.4	22.0	89.0	10.8	26.0	234.3
Degree of fulfilment	0.91	0.25	0.44	0.89	0.43	0.35	

Here, there is one hard return, *Productivity*, weighted at 100, against which the other returns are assessed relatively. To indicate that these returns are not of equal worth, we balance the benefit points, as in Section 3.7. Since the stakeholder group used *parts of the whole* assessment, equalization is not required. (The group did not bother normalizing to keep the total number of benefit points constant between the two tables.)

The returns were subsequently broken down into more specific criteria, as follows.

- Customer satisfaction: achieve a 'very satisfactory' rating in Questback customer reviews.
- Processing time:

- 80% of applications are processed within two days.
- Applications received before July 25 are processed before August 25.
- 70% of applications for payment postponement/waivers are processed within two days.
- All applications for payment postponement/waivers are processed within 26 days.
- Digital dialogue:
  - Clients are 'very satisfied' with the enterprise's digital services in the national inhabitant survey three years from now.
  - At least 98% of all applications for the postponement of payment are web based.
  - At least 90% of all applications to waive interest are web based.
- Productivity: through increased internal productivity, we will release at least EUR 2.5 million from operations to IT systems development on a permanent basis.
- Learning environment and common culture: obtain a minimum score of five on a scale of one to six in the next employee survey on the experience of learning and common culture.
- Expert body: The enterprise provides more facts and assessments of its support schemes and digitization work than at present.

At the time of writing, the intent was to chip off project-specific objectives from these criteria according to the project-level assessments above. Then, the epics within each project were to be assessed on those objectives, as described in the previous chapter.

4.5 The Confirmatory Mode with Open-Ended Worth Points

In Fig. 4.4, note that the worth point totals are not equal for each return. Recall the analogous situation for objectives in Section 3.13 in Chapter 3. Under the assumption that the project objectives together are assumed to contribute fully to the portfolio's planned returns, any difference in worth point totals between returns is an artefact of the estimation method and does not reflect an intentional difference in the degree of fulfilment. Thus, we equalize and normalize the benefit points so that the returns totals are equal, in the same manner as for effect points.

We carry out the equalization by dividing by the total worth points for the return. For example, for project B's $Obj1_B$ on $Ret1$, we have 3/35. We can use the earlier equalize function in Equation (3.5). So, if BP_{jpk} is the amount of worth points for objective j in project P on return k, and BP_k is the total amount of worth points on return k, then the general formula for equalizing worth points is

$$\text{equalize}(BP_{jpk}, BP_k) = BP_{jpk}/BP_k \qquad (4.1)$$

To keep the portfolio worth point total (104 in our case) constant (for cosmetic reasons), one can use the normalize function in Equation (3.3).

Figure 4.8 shows the worth points of our example, equalized and normalized to a total of 104 worth points.

	Ret1	Ret2	Ret3	Total
Project A				
Obj1 $_A$	...	...	...	...
...	...	...	...	...
ObjN $_A$	...	...	...	...
Total A	5.94	18.91	10.59	35
Project B				
Obj1 $_B$	2.97	3.15	4.81	10.94
Obj2 $_B$	2.97	5.25	4.81	13.04
Obj3 $_B$	4.95	1.05	7.70	23.98
Total B	10.90	9.45	17.33	48
Project C				
Obj3 $_C$	...	...	...	...
...	...	...	...	...
ObjN $_C$	...	...	...	...
Total C	17.83	6.30	6.74	31
Total Portfolio	35	35	35	104

Fig. 4.8 A portfolio of three projects with worth points equalized to reflect the total fulfilment of the returns, normalized to 104 total worth points.

Ret1	Ret2	Ret3
5	2	3

Fig. 4.9 Relative assessments of the worth of returns, using Fibonacci numbers.

4.6 Balanced Worth Points

We have been balancing effect points, but we have not balanced worth points. Balancing effect points was necessary to obtain a uniform metric across objectives to order backlogs, and so forth. Worth points were used to compute the weights for the objectives, which were then used to balance effect points. Balancing the worth points themselves has not been necessary.

The main reason for this is that worth points were assessed directly on monetary returns, which automatically applies the same metric (some currency) across returns. However, suppose stakeholders want to use a purely money-independent methodology at this level as well, in line with the basic assumptions of points-based estimation. Figure 4.9 shows the relative assessments of returns, using the Fibonacci scale. These *return points* are an alternative to monetary assessments, even at the strategic level, and we show this for methodological completeness.

In this pure universe of points, one must now balance worth points according to the fact that some returns hold more worth than others. Such a balancing process is analogous to the balancing of effect points, where one multiplies the worth points by the appropriate return's weight (proportion of worth points). For example, in Fig. 4.4, for objective $Obj1_B$ on $Ret1$, 3 * 5/10 for the five return points in Fig. 4.9. So, if BP_{jpk} is the amount of worth points for objective j in project P on return k, and

w_k is the weight of return k, Equation (3.1) gives the formula for balancing effect points, as follows:

$$\text{balance}(BP_{jpk}, w_k) = BP_{jpk} * w_k \qquad (4.2)$$

Again, if you wish to keep the total number of benefit points constant in the portfolio, use the normalize function in Equation (3.3).

Figure 4.10 shows the resulting balanced benefit points for the example in Fig. 4.4. One can see that the resulting weights for the objectives are quite close to those of Fig. 4.2. The differences show that the use of different scales can result in slightly different values. In this context, such variation is not essential, but it is essential to be aware that this is not essential: one must interpret values as rough approximations of cost and benefit. In Chapter 6, we will see how one can express the degree of approximation in terms of uncertainty assessments.

	Ret1	Ret2	Ret3		Weight	
	5	2	3	Total	Project	Enterprise
Project A						
Obj1 $_A$	...	...	...	...	...	...
...	...	...	...	...	...	...
ObjN $_A$	...	...	...	...	...	...
Total A	8.91	11.35	9.53	29.79	1	0.29
Project B						
Obj1 $_B$	4.46	1.89	4.33	10.68	0.28	0.10
Obj2 $_B$	4.46	3.15	4.33	11.94	0.32	0.11
Obj3 $_B$	7.43	0.63	6.93	14.99	0.40	0.14
Total B	16.34	5.67	15.60	37.62	1	0.36
Project C						
Obj1 $_C$	...	...	...	...	...	...
...	...	...	...	...	...	...
ObjN $_C$	...	...	...	...	...	...
Total C	26.74	3.78	6.07	36.59	1	0.35
Total Portfolio	52.00	20.80	31.20	104		1

Fig. 4.10 Benefit points equalized for the total fulfilment of objectives and balanced for the worth of the objectives, normalized to 104 worth points in total.

Chapter 5
Earned Business Value Management

Performance is the best way to shut people up.

MARCUS LEMONIS

Abstract It is time to move on to construction time. This is when epics are distributed to releases and scheduled for further detailing. We use benefit estimates and cost estimates to monitor and adjust this scheduling. We will take an existing practice for cost management and use it for benefit management and benefit/cost management: we adapt what is called *earned value management* to what we call *earned business value management*.

5.1   Introduction

The order in which the project sends its product elements into construction matters. Most organizations must show returns on investment as quickly as possible. Private enterprises must put information technology functionality into production in a way that optimizes earnings as quickly as possible to appease sponsors and other stakeholders; public sector service providers must deploy functionality that quickly provides the intended societal benefit to justify the large public spending in question; and startups survive on timing releases of functionality to appropriately demonstrate outstanding benefit. Various organizations have different goals and objectives for their development projects and portfolios. Moreover, goals and objectives can vary substantially over time (especially for startups [11, 15]). In all of this, it is important to decide what to construct first.

There are several ways to order a backlog, and sophisticated methods and tools exist to do so; that is the substantial topic of release planning. The important point in this book, however, is that, no matter what backlog ordering scheme one uses, projects will fare better if one is aware of the order in which potential benefit is realized. To this end, we will present methods to monitor how much potential benefit one is realizing along the way, in addition to the cost expended. All this can be accomplished by means of benefit estimates, in addition to cost estimates.

The methods in this chapter are particularly suitable, once product element construction is underway in releases. This the stage at which epics are detailed into

J. E. Hannay, *Benefit/Cost-Driven Agile Software Development*,
Simula SpringerBriefs on Computing 8,
https://doi.org/10.1007/978-3-030-74218-8_5

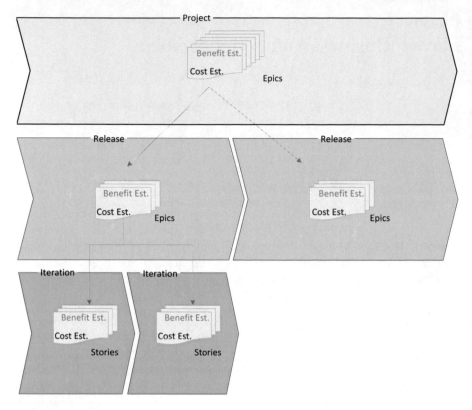

Fig. 5.1 The path to construction. Epics are distributed to releases. When a release is ready to go, its epics are detailed into stories.

stories (see Fig. 5.1). However, the methods can be used at any level of the agile fractal.

5.2 Points for Stories

We use the running example for projects in Chapter 3, specifically the version with Fibonacci numbers (see Figure 3.16 on page 39).

Suppose, now, that the project determines that epics *E3*, *E7*, and *E2* will go into the first release, constructing the most benefit/cost first. In line with *just-in-time* detailing, this is the point at which these epics are elaborated into stories.

Suppose epics *E3*, *E7*, and *E2* are elaborated into stories as indicated in the 'Story' column of Fig. 5.2. Now, also in line with just-in-time thinking, this is when one should assign benefit points and size points to stories.

Epic	Story	BP	Benefit	Part of Epic	BP	Benefit	SP	Cost	Part of Epic	SP	Cost	Benefit/Cost	
E3		23.30	8.45				3.00	1.80				4.69	
	E3A			0.7	16.31	5.91			0.6	1.80	1.08		5.47
	E3B			0.3	6.99	2.53			0.4	1.20	0.72		3.52
E7		28.25	10.24				5.00	3.00				3.41	
	E7A			0.6	16.95	6.15			0.2	1.00	0.60		10.24
	E7B			0.3	8.48	3.07			0.3	1.50	0.90		3.41
	E7C			0.1	2.83	1.02			0.5	2.50	1.50		0.68
E2		45.13	16.36				8.00	4.80				3.41	
	E2A			0.5	22.57	8.18			0.2	1.60	0.96		8.52
	E2B			0.1	4.51	1.64			0.2	1.60	0.96		1.70
	E2C			0.2	9.03	3.27			0.3	2.40	1.44		2.27
	E2D			0.2	9.03	3.27			0.3	2.40	1.44		2.27
E4		17.31	6.28				5.00	3.00				2.09	
E8		26.66	9.67				8.00	4.80				2.01	
E1		24.80	8.99				8.00	4.80				1.87	
E5		30.09	10.91				13.00	7.80				1.40	
E6		15.45	5.60				13.00	7.80				0.72	
Total		211.00	76.50		96.68	35.05	63.00	37.80		16.00	9.60	2.02	3.65

Fig. 5.2 Detailing into stories for the first planned release: epics *E3*, *E7*, and *E2*.

Epic	Story	BP	Benefit	Part of Epic	BP	Benefit	SP	Cost	Part of Epic	SP	Cost	Benefit/Cost	
E4		17.31	6.28				5.00	3.00				2.09	
	E4A			0.3	5.19	1.88			0.2	1.00	0.60		3.14
	E4B			0.2	3.46	1.26			0.3	1.50	0.90		1.39
	E4C			0.3	5.19	1.88			0.4	2.00	1.20		1.57
	E4D			0.2	3.46	1.26			0.1	0.50	0.30		4.18

Fig. 5.3 Detailing into stories for the next epic *E4* in line.

5.2.1 Benefit Points for Stories

We said at the start of this book that considerations of business value should be held at the level of epics, *not* at the level of stories. At the level of stories, one should only consider how much each story contributes to realizing its epic's estimated benefit (see Fig. 5.4). Why? Because stories specify functionality at a level of detail and granularity that usually makes it hard to relate to objectives in the business case [4]. Secondly, it is important to keep expert estimation as local and simple as possible. Therefore, one should consider only one level of the relation at a time: for epics, examine their relation to objectives; for stories, examine their relation to epics.

In this book, we distribute an epic's benefit points to its stories by assessing what proportion of benefit each story is responsible for. This assessment can be performed in various ways (see Section 5.6 for more details). In our example, the results of that task appear in the first column labelled 'Part of Epic' (green numbers on white) in Fig. 5.2, and the resulting portion of the epics' effect benefit points and monetary benefit, respectively, appear in the 'BP' and 'Benefit' columns immediately to the right.

5.2.2 Size Points for Stories

Unlike what we recommend for benefit points, story points are commonly assigned directly at the story and task levels, often by new planning poker sessions conducted by Scrum teams. If subcontractors deliver code to the project, they might also use in-house methods to estimate costs. In any event, costs for stories are not usually estimated by assessing their contribution to the cost of epics. The reason why this is acceptable is that cost estimations retain relevance all the way from strategy to construction, especially when subcontractors are involved at the construction level.

For our techniques, it is advantageous to express size points for stories in terms of the proportions of the epic's size points (Fig. 5.4), since this enables one to relate directly to epics. Story size points can be expressed in this way, regardless of how they are actually assigned to stories. For our example, we will assume the proportions of story points for epics as in the second 'Part of Epic' column (red numbers on white) of Fig. 5.2 and the resulting portion of the epic's cost in the 'SP' and 'Cost' columns to the right.

5.3 Ordering the Story Backlog

In Fig. 5.2, we note that, although the three epics *E3*, *E7*, and *E2* selected for the first release are those expected to deliver the most benefit for cost, the individual stories within them might not all be as beneficial. Note that story *E7C* has an unfortunate benefit-cost ratio and should probably not be put into construction.

The basic principle for ordering the story backlog is straightforward: order the backlog according to decreasing benefit/cost. If one puts stories into construction in that order, the next story in line will always be the one that is foreseen to generate the most benefit relative to cost in the remaining backlog. If one plots the accumulated estimated benefit against the accumulated estimated cost as one puts the backlog into construction, one obtains a realization curve with a steep incline that eases off, revealing a plan to generate benefit potential faster than cost potential. See Fig. 5.5 for our example. This is the tactic of maximizing the benefit-cost ratio, that is, promoting the benefit/cost factor as the most important in the benefit/cost triangle in Fig. 2.8.

Fig. 5.4 Proportions of the epic's benefit points and story points distributed on stories.

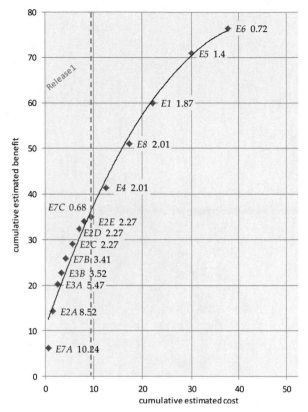

Fig. 5.5 Planned realization curve for the release left of the green line. The remainder of the queue (unelaborated epics) is to the right of the green line. Benefit/cost values are in blue.

One should assess the information that is available at any point of time, and one should always consider revising the plan. Already now one could plan to drop *E7C* from the current release. One would then have the available capacity in the release to do something more useful. Suppose we take the time to elaborate the next epic, *E4*, in the prioritized line and that we have the stories as shown in Fig. 5.3. In place of the 1.5 for the cost for *E7C*, one can plan to spend 0.9 on *E4D* and *E4A*, the two most benefit/cost-efficient stories in this next epic. They have a total estimated benefit of 3.14. If one only has cost for guidance, one could be tempted to fill up the planned capacity of the first release by a full cost of 1.5 by choosing, say, *E4C* and *E4D*, but this would just yield the same benefit at higher cost. Figure 5.6 shows the revised plan, where *E7C* has been bumped down the line and out of this release and where *E4D* and *E4A* have been included in the release instead. Figure 5.7 shows the cumulative values of the ordered stories in this revised release. We will discuss the results in the two rightmost columns in Fig. 5.7 shortly.

In taking advantage of the available capacity as we just did, we used an alternative tactic, namely, the maximization of business value within a fixed cost. This approach

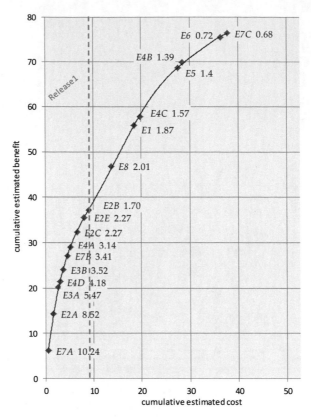

Fig. 5.6 Planned realization curve for the revised release to the left of green line. The remainder of the queue is to the right of the green line. The benefit/cost values are in blue.

is a variant of the *knapsack problem*, which is inherent to release planning. So, given an overall tactic for the project of maximizing benefit/cost, one might have to adhere to a fixed cost bound when adjusting a given release, thereby relating temporarily to the agile triangle rather than the benefit/cost triangle (Fig. 2.8).

   In an attempt to optimize the plan at this stage, one could now elaborate all epics and find the most benefit/cost-efficient stories from the remaining suite of epics, inserting these into the free capacity of the release. This would require one to invest more cost earlier – to elaborate the epics – when project experience and knowledge is potentially lower than at a later stage. This is, as it sounds, against agile principles. Still, the epics must be elaborated at some point, and the decision of when to do so is a nuance of whatever tactic one is following. We cannot answer when exactly the best time would be to elaborate epics. The point we are making is that these techniques should help the project make better-informed decisions on such issues.

Story	BP	Benefit	Cumulative SP	Cost	AB	AC
E7A	16.95	6.15	1.00	0.60	6.15	1.20
E2A	39.52	14.33	2.60	1.56	10.24	2.54
E3A	55.83	20.24	4.40	2.64	16.15	2.87
E4D	59.29	21.50	4.90	2.94	17.40	3.77
E3B	66.28	24.03	6.10	3.66	19.94	5.21
E7B	74.75	27.10	7.60	4.56	23.01	6.11
E4A	79.95	28.99	8.60	5.16	24.89	7.01
E2C	88.97	32.26	11.00	6.60	28.17	11.33
E2D	98.00	35.53	13.40	8.04		
E2B	102.51	37.17	15.00	9.00		

Fig. 5.7 Stories in first revised release sorted by decreasing benefit/cost. This table shows the cumulative points and monetary values for the cost and benefit estimates and the actual or adjusted cost and adjusted benefit.

5.4 Monitor Earned Business Value

The use of the metrics of *earned value management* (EVM) is a common way of measuring a project's efficiency. Generally, EVM relies on having the means to quantify work done. Agile accommodates this nicely through its product elements and product backlog.

But brace yourself, because one uses the term *value* in the EVM regime in a way that confounds cost with value, which is truly unfortunate, since people tend to believe that costlier things inherently have more value [1]. In the following, we will therefore be rather pedantic regarding the clarity of terms.

Consider, then, the project in some period p at the end of which you have decided to assess project efficiency. The period can represent a sprint, a release, or the entire project up until now. Then, we define the following metrics:

- *Planned value PV* is the estimated cost of the product elements planned for completion in p.
- *Earned value EV* is the estimated cost of those product elements that are actually completed in p.
- *Actual or adjusted cost AC* is the cost of the product elements that were completed in p. If the cost estimates are for development only, then AC is the actual cost incurred developing the product elements. If the cost estimates are for life cycle costs, and life cycle costs are assumed to be proportional by a factor L to development cost, then AC is the actual development cost multiplied by L. Since AC in the latter case retains an estimate element, one can call this the *adjusted cost* rather than the actual cost.
- *Cost performance index CPI* $= EV/AC$.

Figure 5.8 illustrates the above metrics for our example. The period in question is the first release, and we planned to produce 10 stories, *E7A* to *E2B*, with a total

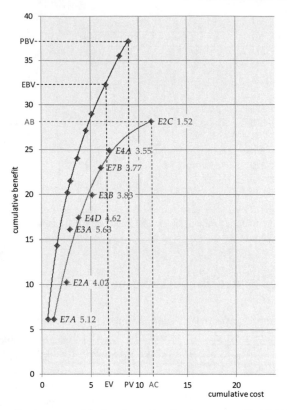

Fig. 5.8 Planned realization curve (blue) and actual realization curve with AB/AC values (orange) for each story, first release.

estimated cost $PV = 9.00$ (from Fig. 5.7). However, the project only managed to complete the first eight stories, *E7A* to *E2C*, in time. The total cost estimate for these eight stories is $EV = 6.60$. At this point, we have the actual development cost for these eight stories, say, 5.665. Assuming, for this example, that the life cycle cost is proportional by a factor of two to development cost, the adjusted cost for the eight stories is $AC = 11.33$ (from Fig. 5.7). The project is therefore both behind schedule and above the planned cost. We find that $CPI = 6.60/11.33 = 0.58$ is well below one. A *CPI* value below one indicates that productivity is lower than anticipated, and the obvious recommendation for a low *CPI* value is to take action so that one obtains a better *CPI* the next period.

As much sense as that makes, the CPI is merely a measure of how much functionality is being produced, not how valuable that functionality is. EVM is designed to support management by the iron triangle (Fig. 2.8, left panel). Therefore, we define the following explicit metrics for *earned benefit management*, or *earned business value management* to counter the terminology of EVM:

- *Planned business value PBV* is the estimated business value of the product elements planned for in p.
- *Earned business value EBV* is the estimated business value of the product elements completed in p.
- *Adjusted benefit AB* is the re-estimated business value of the product elements completed in p.
- *Benefit performance index BPI = EBV/AB*.
- *Benefit cost performance index BCPI = EBV/AC*.
- *Adjusted benefit cost ABC = AB/AC*.

In our example, $PBV = 37.17$ and $EBV = 32.26$ (from Fig. 5.7). Although EBV is less than PBV, we have $BCPI = 32.26/11.33 = 2.85$, which is well above one. A $BCPI$ value below unity means that one is investing more money than one is expecting to gain, and, in this case, one should consider alternative investments. A cleverly prioritized project will start with a high $BCPI$, earning a large amount of business value compared to the cost expended in the beginning of the project. Here, after the first release, the project's velocity with regards to cost is not good, but the project's velocity with regards to business value is acceptable relative to cost. Such balanced information is important when reporting to organization management and project and product owners, but it is also important for virtually every stakeholder of the project, because it provides a wider picture that includes the progress in terms of customer value, and not only in the amount of functionality.

In traditional EVM, *Actual cost* is the expenditure for development. We have generalized this to *adjusted cost* to account for post-deployment costs, which have not yet been incurred. For our earned business value management (EBVM) regime, we define the analogous *Adjusted benefit AB*, which is a re-estimate of benefit based on experience from using increments deployed from the project or from other re-estimates of benefit due to, for example, changes in external factors, such as legislation and dependencies on the evolution of other systems. For our example, let us imagine that *E2A* was found to be overrated, once stakeholders saw the story's functionality in action, and was subsequently re-estimated to half its original benefit. We can therefore write $AB = 28.17$ (from Fig. 5.7), which yields $BPI = 32.26/28.17 = 1.15$. The term BPI is a pure business value metric, and values greater than one mean that the project is generating less business value than expected. Still, the *Adjusted benefit cost ABC* $= 28.17/11.33 = 2.49$, so we are faring quite well.

One can further derive several other metrics from the basic metrics of EVM and EBVM. We can then construct our own dashboard for monitoring project efficiency in terms of cost and benefit. You can see that benefit points and story points are at the core of how we define the EVM and EBVM metrics here. It can be advantageous to make benefit points and story points even more explicit (see Section 5.8). Benefit points and story points provide the means of defining a host of metrics that tap directly into one's construction line, which also has meaningful indications in terms of the business case.

5.5 Wrapping Up

With both story points and benefit points in your vocabulary, you can enhance your capability to systematize project knowledge and project learning on aspects that matter the most, namely, those of business value. Here, we showed how to order the product backlog and keep track of productivity in terms of not only cost, but also business value. In that light, it is pertinent to ask how one would consider running projects aimed at delivering value for the customer, based on the metrics of cost alone. In another discussion, we will show how risk and uncertainty can be integrated into this approach.

5.6* Assigning Benefit Points to Stories

Benefit estimation for a story should not relate directly to objectives, but indirectly via the benefit points of its epic. We have suggested syntax for epics that explicitly mentions objectives [8]. Here, to help you think of stories in terms of their contribution to their epic, you can use the following syntax, where the objectives are explicitly not mentioned:

> Story: *As* <stakeholder A> *I can* <perform actions d in domain D> *by using* <functionality f in system S> *to* <perform actions s in S> *in order to* <contribute to Epic E>

One can be faced with more stories than one can comfortably keep track of when distributing benefit points from an epic. The solution? Use available distribution techniques, based on assessing relative importance. We compared four possible techniques in an experiment [3, 2], which led to the recommendation of pairwise comparison, facilitated by the analytical hierarchy process (AHP) [13], which is easily implemented in a tool. The comparison of many items in one go is cognitively extremely taxing. Instead, AHP is based on the principle of considering only two items at a time by assessing their relative importance. Surely, however, this extremely local procedure completely ignores the whole picture and all the inter-item relations. Yes and no. Given one's assessment of two items at a time, the AHP algorithm deduces a ranking of all the items. The essential detail is that the AHP produces a ranking even in the face of inconsistencies. Unless you have extraordinary capabilities, your local pairwise comparisons will likely imply $EX > EY$ and, at the same time, $EY > EX$ for some stories EX and *EY*. The AHP computes a measure for this inconsistency, the consistency index. In line with *satisficing*, rather than optimizing [16], one can make an educated choice as to a 'good enough' consistency index. In standard AHP, all possible pairs of stories in an epic must be compared, which can be overcomeable for a moderate number of stories. In our experiments, we implemented a method to reduce the number of comparisons required [10] (with the penalty of having to be more consistent), so that AHP could also be used for large numbers of stories.

Pairwise comparison is a core element of cognitive judgement processes [12]. Using a method that directly supports one's cognitive processes is a good way to obtain better expert estimates.

5.7* Dependencies

Functional, temporal, and architectural dependencies between product elements are common. In addition, worldly factors such as available expertise, illness, conflicts, external constraints, and so forth can all be influential when stories are put into construction.

We do not treat dependencies as such in this book, and it is important to realize that the perfectly benefit/cost-ordered backlog is an input to the release planning stage, where dependencies are dealt with in full. Our approach is integral to more detailed dependency handling. For example, Cleland-Huang and Denne [7] give a thorough account of the consequences that dependencies have on cost and benefit realization, and they present a heuristic that approximates the optimal ordering of dependency-heavy product elements with respect to return on value in a net present value regime. Assigning points to product elements would provide the necessary cost and benefit estimates prior to applying such heuristics. Due to dependencies, one's backlog might end up differently than perfectly benefit/cost-ordered, but because benefit points and story points are assigned, one can track the project's planned and actual productivity, even in the turmoil of dependency-driven release planning.

With that said, we claim that dependencies can also be the result of unhealthy architectural work and divisions of functionality into pieces that do not make operational sense. The focus on organizational agility has brought forth concepts such as minimum marketable features, minimum business increments, and minimum viable products. All these notions embody minimal product elements that add value for the customer, the flip side of the coin being that a product element involved in dependencies does not bring value in and of itself. Further, the present focus on capabilities and services [18, 6] stresses the development of independent pieces of functionality that persist over time and in multiple contexts at both the business and technical levels [9]. If one is in line with these architectural modes, then, whenever strong dependencies arise, one can take the opportunity to reconsider how functionality is divided. For example, product elements that exhibit strong dependencies can more sensibly be combined into one element.

5.8* Agile EBVM in Practice

When applying EBVM, we have found it useful to relate to alternative but equivalent expressions for *CPI* and *BCPI* that clearly separate points and monetary value.

Although less streamlined in definition than the expressions in the main text, our experience is that project stakeholders intuitively understand these metrics better and that they increase the transparency of the project state. They stimulate one to use EBVM based purely on points and on monetary expressions that are more accessible, such as total budgeted cost and benefit. We have found the effort required to collect data and calculate the metrics to be almost negligible. You will likely need to try this out in practice, for example, in a spreadsheet, to get a handle on the larger numbers of expressions, but once you have done so, we think you might find this way simpler. Consider the following definitions for a given period p:

- PSP, the planned size points,
- ESP, the earned size points,
- TSP, the total number of size points assigned in the project, and
- $FSP = ESP/TSP$, the proportion of the total number of size points that is earned.

In our example, the period in question is the first (revised) release (Figs. 5.7 and 5.8), and $PSP = 15$, $ESP = 11$, and TSP $= 63$. Then, $FSP = 11/63 = 17.5\%$. Further, consider the following definitions:

- VSP, the monetary value of a size point used for the period,
- $TPV = TSP * VSP$, the estimated total life cycle cost – or total planned value – given VSP, and
- $FC = AC/TPV$, the proportion of total planned value that is committed.

In our example, $VSP = 0.6$ million, $TPV = 37.80$ million, and $FC = 11.33/37.80 = 29.97\%$. With simple math, one can verify that

- $CPI = FSP/FC$

For our example, $CPI = 17.5/29.97 = 0.58$, the same as calculated earlier the standard way.

Now, consider the following definitions for a given period p;

- PBP, the planned benefit points,
- EBP, the earned benefit points,
- TBP, the total number of benefit points assigned in the project, and
- $FBP = EBP/TBP$, the proportion of the total number of benefit points that is earned.

In our example (Figs. 5.7 and 5.8) $PBP = 102.51$, $EBP = 88.97$, and TBP $= 211$. Then, $FBP = 88.97/211 = 42.17\%$. Further, consider the following:

- VBP, the monetary value of a benefit point used for the period.
- $TPBV = TBP * VBP$, the estimated total life cycle benefit – or total planned business value – given VBP, and
- $FB = AB/TPBV$, the proportion of total planned business value that is committed.

In our example, $VBP = 0.36$ million, $TPBV = 76.50$ million, and $FB = 28.17/76.5 = 36.82\%$. It is easy to verify that

- $BPI = FBP/FB$ and
- $BCPI = FBP/FC * TPBV/TPV$.

For our example, $BPI = 42.17/36.82 = 1.15$ and $BCPI = 42.17/29.97 * 76.50/37.80 = 1.41 * 2.02 = 2.85$, the same as calculated earlier the standard way.

Some of the cost metrics (SP, ESP, TSP, VSP, TPV) are in line with ideas in, for example, [5, 17, 14]. The VSP is often understood as the budgeted baseline cost per story point fixed throughout the project. However, you can also choose to have a dynamic VSP reflecting project experience, depending on what kind of agile you are committed to. You can even equip your dashboard with a fixed VSP and a dynamic VSP, and the same applies for VBP, of course.

References

1. D. Ariely, Ed., *Predictably Irrational: The Hidden Forces That Shape Our Decisions*. Harper Perennial, 2010.
2. H.C. Benestad and J.E. Hannay, "A comparison of model-based and judgment-based release planning in incremental software projects," in *Proc. 33rd Int'l Conf. Software Engineering (ICSE 2011)*. ACM, 2011, pp. 766–775.
3. H.C. Benestad and J.E. Hannay, "Does the prioritization technique affect stakeholders' selection of essential software product features?" *Proc. 6th Int'l Symp. Empirical Software Engineering and Measurement (ESEM)*, pp. 261–270, 2012.
4. M. Cohn, *Agile Estimating and Planning*. Prentice Hall, 2005.
5. CollabNet, "Monitoring Scrum projects with agile EVM and earned business value measures," 2013.
6. M.H. Danesh and E. Yu, "Analyzing IT flexibility to enable dynamic capabilities," in *Advanced Information Systems Engineering Workshops*, ser. Lecture Notes in Business Information Processing. Springer, 2015, vol. 215, pp. 53–65.
7. M. Denne and J. Cleland-Huang, "The incremental funding method: Data-driven software development," *IEEE Software*, vol. 21, no. 3, pp. 39–47, May/June 2004.
8. J.E. Hannay, H.C. Benestad, and K. Strand, "Earned business value management—see that you deliver value to your customer," *IEEE Software*, vol. 34, no. 4, pp. 58–70, 2017.
9. J.E. Hannay, K. Brathen, and O.M. Mevassvik, "Agile requirements handling in a service-oriented taxonomy of capabilities," *Requirements Engineering*, vol. 22, no. 2, pp. 289–314, 2017.
10. P.T. Harker, "Incomplete pairwise comparisons in the analytic hierarchy process," *Mathematical Modelling*, vol. 9, no. 11, pp. 837–848, 1987.
11. G.A. Moore, *Inside the Tornado*, revised ed. Harper Business, 2004.
12. T. Mussweiler, "Comparison processes in social judgment: Mechanisms and consequences," *Psych. Review*, vol. 110, no. 3, pp. 472–489, 2003.
13. A. Perini, F. Ricca, and A. Susi, "Tool-supported requirements prioritization: Comparing the AHP and CBRank methods," *Information and Software Technology*, vol. 51, no. 6, pp. 1021–1032, 2009.
14. D. Rawsthorne, "Calculating earned business value for an agile project," http://www.danube.com/system/files/CollabNet_WP_Earned_Business_Value_041910.pdf, 2010, accessed May 2013.
15. E.M. Rogers, *Diffusion of Innovations*, 5th ed. Free Press, 2003.
16. H.A. Simon, *The Sciences of the Artificial*, 3rd ed. MIT Press, 1996.
17. T. Sulaiman, B. Barton, and T. Blackburn, "AgileEVM— earned value management in Scrum projects," in *Proc. IEEE AGILE 2006*. IEEE Computer Society, 2006, pp. 7–16.
18. The Open Group, *SOA Reference Architecture Technical Standard*, 2011, doc. no. C119.

Chapter 6
Agile Uncertainty Assessment for Benefit Points and Size Points

We demand rigidly defined areas of doubt and uncertainty!

DOUGLAS ADAMS, *The Hitchhiker's Guide to the Galaxy*

Abstract Agile methodology purports to deal with uncertainty through continuous monitoring and learning. To do so, we need to see how productivity is faring against our plans, as in the previous chapter. But we also need to communicate what our uncertainty is realistically. This is regularly done for cost, but must also be done for benefit to obtain a complete picture. In this chapter, we show how both benefit points and size points can be instantiated with values reflecting different levels of uncertainty.

6.1 Introduction

A very fortunate thing about points-based estimates is that one can instantiate them with different values that reflect the stakeholders' current understanding. We instantiated the points with initial monetary values in Fig. 3.16. We will instantiate points with values that reflect scenarios according to uncertainty assessments.

In particular, we will demonstrate how to instantiate points with so-called pX values, where the p stands for percentile. If you are looking at a set of project outcome values, a pX value is the boundary value above or equal to $X\%$ of all sorted outcome values. So, if one has a database of historical data with actual cost outcomes, and one sorts those projects on descending cost, the p85 value for cost is the value below which one finds 85% of the projects. Equivalently, one finds 15% of the projects above that value.

In the unlikely event that the database also has historical data on benefit, the p35 value, say, would be the benefit value below which one finds 35% of the projects when sorted on descending benefit. Equivalently, one finds 65% of the projects above that value.

J. E. Hannay, *Benefit/Cost-Driven Agile Software Development*,
Simula SpringerBriefs on Computing 8,
https://doi.org/10.1007/978-3-030-74218-8_6

6.2   Uncertainty Assessment

In this section, we want to estimate the most likely benefit and most likely cost of a new project, together with upper and lower bounds due to uncertainty. In [2], one can see how to derive pX values from relevant historical project outcome data, to provide cost estimates for a project.

However, historical data are often not available. In particular, outcome data in terms of benefit are currently extremely sparse. In this situation, one can elicit and systematize the stakeholders' perception of uncertainty. To do so, one should address the drivers of uncertainty that the stakeholders identify as salient to the project.

One can sort drivers of uncertainty into two categories: estimation uncertainty and event uncertainty. The former reflects the fact that estimates are forecasts of the future and are therefore inherently uncertain. In our context, we have estimates of

- A product element's lifecycle cost,
- A product element's effect on objectives, and
- An objective's worth on returns.

To assess estimation uncertainty is to contemplate the inherent uncertainty associated with these estimates. Event uncertainty, on the other hand, pertains to uncertainty arising from events internal and external to the project. Contemplating event uncertainty involves *risk assessments*. Risk assessment is another extensive subject that the reader should review elsewhere.

Here, we are out to express, simplistically, the resulting perception of uncertainty, however the group of stakeholders arrived at it. We will exemplify with three-point estimates.

Let us first look at cost estimates, since this is common practice in many organizations. We choose to express estimation uncertainty at the level of epics. However, our stakeholders might find it more meaningful to assess uncertainty on groups of epics or on other parts of the current backlog. It is possible to assess uncertainty at lower levels of the product breakdown structure if that is meaningful in the context in question.

Let us assume that the appropriate stakeholders have come up with the relative cost estimates in Fig. 3.8 (p. 29), and that they have used their knowledge and experience to fix the initial monetary value of a size point at 0.6 million, producing an estimate of 37.8 million for the most likely project development and post-deployment cost, as shown in the 'Cost' column of Fig. 3.16 (p. 39).

The stakeholders have devised three-point uncertainty cost estimates for the epics and events given in the upper half of Fig. 6.1. Note that the most likely cost estimates for epics are those in Fig. 3.16.[1] For example, for epic *E3*, the most likely estimate is 1.8 million (corresponding to Fig. 3.16). This epic also has a bad-case estimate

---

[1] Note, also, that the three-point estimates are in terms of monetary values, not size points. Conceptually, three-point estimates could well belong in the realm of size points and benefit points. However, the task of assessing uncertainty on abstract points is not feasible in practice, unless one has historical data to derive uncertainty intervals in terms of percentages, for example. Here, we emphasize an approach that allows us to assess uncertainty from scratch.

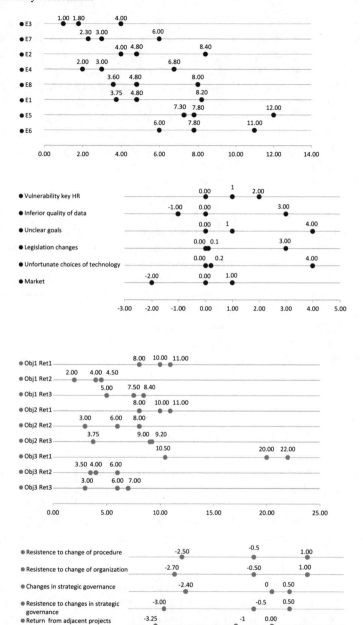

Fig. 6.1 Three-point estimates for cost are in red, and those for benefit in green. The figure shows both the estimation uncertainty and event uncertainty.

of four and a good-case estimate of one. Further, the three-point estimate for *E2* is wider than that for *E3*, indicating lower confidence in the most likely estimate. All the three-point estimates are asymmetrical, reflecting the fact that the range of probable outcomes stretches further upward than downward.

Next, for the three-point estimates of event uncertainty in Fig. 6.1, a value of zero signifies that the event, if it occurs, will have no impact, while negative values signify that the event could lead to a decrease in cost, and positive values signify that the event could lead to an increase in cost. Most of the event uncertainties are assessed to increase cost, but, for this example, 'Market and Inferior quality of data' are assessed to provide probabilities of decreasing cost.

For uncertainty regarding benefit, in the example, we choose to show the uncertainty assessment on the worth relation, in other words, the objectives' contribution to return. See, for example, Fig. 4.2 (p. 51). Figure 6.1 (bottom half) illustrates such assessments. For example, for the *Obj3–Ret1* relation, the most likely estimate is 20 million (0.2*100 million in Fig. 4.2), with an upper bound of 22 and a lower bound of 10. Figure 6.1 also shows examples of event uncertainty assessments for benefit.

In contrast to the estimates for cost, the three-point estimates reflect the expectation that the ranges of probable outcomes of benefit tend to stretch farther downward than upward. Again, one can assess uncertainty at any level that makes sense in a given project. For example, one could assess uncertainty on the effect relation instead of, or in addition to, the worth relation. In this example, we assume that stakeholders' perceptions of uncertainty are more salient at a level closer to the business domain.

6.3 Use of Uncertainty Assessments

A three-point estimate gives a range of probable values, which is an important step in acknowledging that hitting the target on a single estimate is not a realistic goal. By itself, though, a three-point estimate does not indicate how probable different values are. For that, one needs a probability distribution. If one has usable theoretical or empirical results, one might be able to apply these results to choose an appropriate distribution type. For example, theoretically, time and cost are often distributed lognormally, as illustrated in Fig. 6.2.

In software projects one is often not in a position to apply theoretical results, and the best bet is to use rule-of-thumb methods that are good enough. The *project evaluation and review techniques* (PERT) [5] includes one such method, where one calculates an expected value estimate *EV* from a three-point estimate as $EV=(low+4*most\ likely+high)/6$. This approach assumes a beta distribution (see Fig. 6.2, middle panel).

Even simpler, a triangular distribution is given by the formula for the area of a triangle (see Fig. 6.2, bottom panel), which could be a better approximation when one is not able to apply theory or empirical data.

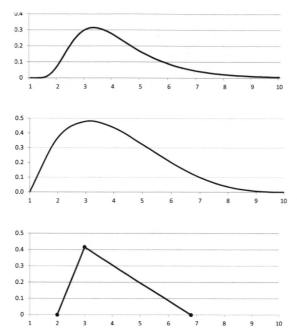

Fig. 6.2 Example of probability distributions based on the three-point cost estimates for epic *E4*: lognormal (top), beta (middle), and triangular (bottom).

The low and high values in the three-point estimates can have various interpretations. For example, when experts naturally think in terms of 'in one of 10 cases with epics similar to this one, the cost will be less than *low*, and in nine of 10 cases the cost will be less than *high*', it is the p10 (*low*) and P90 (*high*) values for the epic that are being estimated. The PERT method, on the other hand, prompts for low and high values without asking for probabilities, which could be advantageous, since thinking in terms of probabilities is hard [3, 6]. The triangular distribution interprets the low and high values simply as p0 and p100 values.

Exactly what marginal probabilities your low and high values represent is not that important. It is more important that your interval is not too narrow. According to evidence [1], you should fix the low and high values first and then assess the probability of staying within these bounds, rather than fix a probability first and then find an interval in which there is that probability of staying within the interval. Research is ongoing on how best to elicit people's perceptions of uncertainty.

6.4 Obtaining p*X* Values for the Project

We now want to use the above assessments on uncertainty drivers to construct project-wide p*X* values that we can plug into our benefit points and size points.

For simplicity, we will use the triangular distributions generated automatically from the three-point estimates in Fig. 6.1, and we will assume that the drivers are independent of each other. These distributions are then given as input to Monte Carlo simulations.[2]

A Monte Carlo simulation simulates a large number of project runs, say, 10,000, and it will do so based on our uncertainty assessments expressed as probability distributions. One simulated run will capture one possible project outcome according to one draw of the hat from each of the supplied distributions. Over a large number of runs, the more likely values, according to the distributions, will be drawn more frequently. This, in turn, will affect the distribution of total project outcomes.

Figure 6.3 (top) shows the histogram after 60,000 iterations giving the proportion of times the simulation outcome fell within a given cost interval (with intervals of 0.25 million each).

The cumulative curve of the histogram (Fig. 6.3, second panel) is generated by adding the bar heights in the histogram from left to right and plotting the result. One can then easily read off the project-level pX values. See Section 6.7 for common values. The p50 most likely cost estimate is 49.25 million, here, giving a size point value of 0.78 million. The p85 bad-case estimate is 52.75 million, which yields a size point of 0.84 million. The p35 good-case estimate is 48.00 million, for a size point value of 0.71 million.

Example 1. Some early adopters have also applied this approach in benefit estimates, as advocated in the main text. For example, a large business-critical Norwegian public agency analyzed possible changes to business processes within one of their service domains. It then estimated the benefit of each change, including uncertainty assessments, by providing three-point estimates of the time that could be saved in the processes due to the planned changes. These estimates were converted to monetary values and submitted as triangular distributions to Monte Carlo simulation. The project could therefore provide a range within which the benefit for the functional domain would arise, together with pX estimates.

This organization also developed a dashboard for tracking earned business value along the lines described in the previous chapter. They are not yet applying the practice of using benefit points, but when they do, they will be able to view different scenarios concurrently in the dashboard by plugging various pX values into their points.

---

[2] There will be dependencies. Product elements are independent, in that they can provide individual benefits, but they will likely depend on each other for maximum effect. Additionally, event uncertainty drivers will likely be interdependent, and so on. Modelling dependencies and their effects is outside the scope of this text and described elsewhere. The independence assumption is reasonable if coarse-grained drivers are used as input for the Monte Carlo simulations, and one can still carry out meaningful uncertainty assessments for the *main* effects under this assumption.

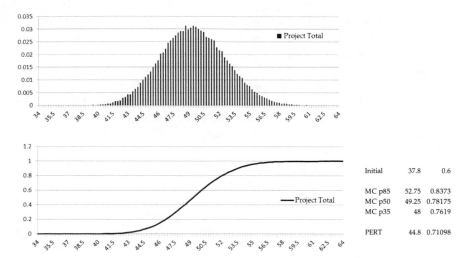

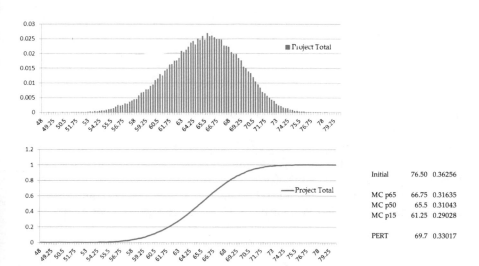

Fig. 6.3 Monte Carlo simulations of cost (red) and benefit (green), with histograms and cumulative curves.

Looking again at the histogram (Fig. 6.3 top), it is not at all likely for cost to be as low as the initial project estimate of 37.8 million calculated prior to uncertainty assessment. Further, the PERT approach would involve computing the PERT expected value for each three-point estimate in Fig. 6.1 and adding them to obtain a project total of 44.8 million, within which the project only has about a 7.5% chance of staying.

Regarding benefit, Fig. 6.3 (bottom half) shows the histogram after 60,000 iterations, giving the proportion of times the simulation outcome fell within a given benefit interval (with intervals of 0.25 million each). The cumulative curve (bottom) indicates that the p50 most likely estimate is 65.5 million (1 benefit point = 0.31 million), the p15 bad-case estimate is 61.25 million (1 benefit point = 0.29 million), and the p65 good-case estimate is 66.75 million (1 benefit point = 0.32 million). According to the histogram, there is zero likelihood of obtaining the initial project estimate of 76.5 million or better, and only about a 0.12% chance of obtaining the PERT estimate of 69.7 million or better.

This is a fictitious example, and pX estimates will not necessarily give more pessimistic forecasts than initial base estimates. However, the example demonstrates that, if the project does have a perception of uncertainty, one should capture it by using, for example, three-point estimates and a sound method for integrating these uncertainty assessments into the base estimates (e.g. using Monte Carlo simulations). The use of base estimates alone ignores project knowledge. Research also shows that the PERT method as such can lead one astray [4], but that the beta distribution it is based on can be used sensibly in Monte Carlo simulations.

6.5   Instantiation with pX Values

Now we are ready to instantiate benefit points and size points with pX values. Figure 6.4 shows the benefit/cost according to initial estimates and the good-case, most likely, and bad-case pX estimates. Figure 6.5 shows the corresponding planned realization curves.

So, a project manager who has been given the p65/p35 order should work with monetary values of 0.32 million for benefit points and 0.71 million for size points. If you are allowed to work with p50 estimates, then you should use 0.31 million for benefit points and 0.78 million for size points. Both choices will impact when to stop construction and affect how backlogs are prioritized across a portfolio.

6.6   Simple Sensitivity Analysis

Looking more closely at the p50 scenario compared to the initial estimates, we find the estimates imply that *E5* joins *E6* in being questionable for construction. If your stakeholders' uncertainty assessments were different, your p50 estimates might be providing an overall stronger benefit-to-cost ratio than your initial estimates, making *E6* more viable. At this point, however, you can see what happens if you were to eliminate waste by discarding *E6* from the plan. In reality, you would wait until story elaboration time to eliminate waste, but it is still strategically useful to experiment at the level of epics.

	Benefit/Cost			
	Initial	p65/p35	p50	p15/p85
E3	4.69	3.22	3.08	2.69
E7	3.41	2.35	2.24	1.96
E2	3.41	2.34	2.24	1.96
E4	2.09	1.44	1.37	1.20
E8	2.01	1.38	1.32	1.16
E1	1.87	1.29	1.23	1.07
E5	1.40	0.96	0.92	0.80
E6	0.72	0.49	0.47	0.41
total	2.02	1.39	1.33	1.16

Fig. 6.4 Benefit/cost obtained by instantiating benefit points and size points with initial estimates, good-case estimates (p65 for benefit, p35 for cost), expected case estimates (p50 for both benefit and cost), and bad-case estimates (p15 for benefit, p85 for cost). Bad benefit-cost ratios are outlined in red, and questionable ones in yellow.

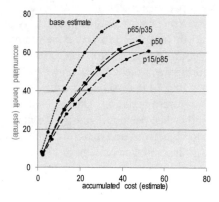

Fig. 6.5 Planned realization curves. Accumulated planned benefit is plotted against accumulated planned cost.

The point to be made here is that you can run Monte Carlo simulations on your initial estimates with uncertainty assessments again, but omitting *E6*. In this example, you obtain a p50 benefit point value of 0.32 million on the remaining 195.55 benefit points and a p50 size point value of 0.82 on the remaining 50 size points. The use of these values to recompute your epics backlog benefit-cost ratios still renders *E5* as waste. Now, you can try eliminating *E5* instead, since *E5* has a cost uncertainty assessment that tends towards higher values (Fig. 6.1). Recomputing p50 estimates renders *E6* as waste. You can try eliminating both *E6* and *E5* and re-computing the p50 estimates, which produces a backlog without waste at the level of epics. Figure 6.6 (top) summarizes this sensitivity analysis and waste elimination with the relevant values.

You can carry out this exercise even if you do not use uncertainty assessments. Then, you simply eliminate the epic with an unfortunate benefit-cost ratio (*E6*), and you are done (Fig. 6.6, bottom panel).

	per BP	per SP	Ratio	Benefit Total	Cost Total	Ratio Total	Waste
MC p50	0.31	0.78	0.397	65.50	49.25	1.330	E6 (0.47), E5 (0.92)
MCp50 E6 eliminated	0.32	0.82	0.396	63.50	41.00	1.549	E5 (0.92)
MCp50 E5 eliminated	0.34	0.81	0.422	61.50	40.25	1.528	E6 (0.50)
MCp50 E6 & E5 eliminated	0.36	0.86	0.416	59.50	32.00	1.859	no waste

	per BP	per SP	Ratio	Benefit Total	Cost Total	Ratio Total	Waste
Initial	0.36	0.60	0.604	76.50	37.80	2.024	E6 (0.72)
E6 eliminated	0.36	0.60	0.604	70.90	30.00	2.363	no waste

Fig. 6.6 Eliminating waste based on p50 estimates (top panel) and initial estimates (bottom panel).

To incorporate uncertainty or not is a choice that has to made based on how much effort one wishes to expend on project governance and on how meaningfully stakeholders think they can assess uncertainty. If you incorporate uncertainty into your project metrics, you can enhance project learning, both by making uncertainty an explicit – and acceptable – part of project life and by adjusting your numbers and plans to reflect uncertainty. You can use simple uncertainty assessment methods to generate pX estimates that you can plug into your benefit points and size points, giving you various views on your project that you can report to your stakeholders. You can do this at any point during the project, based on whatever is left of your backlog or portions of it. Regarding benefit uncertainty, we illustrated the use of three-point estimates for the objective–returns relation. During construction, you have to adjust the amount of return that has been realized by the partly achieved objectives. Since benefit points map to objectives, and therefore returns, this adjustment can be computed automatically, a substantial advantage of using benefit points.

6.7* How Businesses Construct Project-Level pX Values

Over the years, it has become common practice to provide uncertainty analyses for cost in large public sector projects in Norway. Such analyses are mandatory for projects above NOK 750 million (about USD 100 million), but smaller projects, down to NOK 10 million, also perform these analyses. There is work underway to establish benefit budget regimes analogous to those for cost. The corresponding pX values for benefit uncertainty reserves could be given in terms of, for example, p50 (for the project owner), p15 (bad case), and p65 (for the project manager).

The following is a common approach for cost estimates. A similar approach can be used for benefit estimates.

1. Estimation uncertainty:

   a. Walk through the project scenario and identify drivers for estimation uncertainty in the initial cost baseline. It is common to choose drivers of a certain size, such as groups of epics, so that the total number of drivers will be less than 15.

    b. For each driver, provide three-point estimates:

        i. Optimistic scenario – what will be the lowest cost in one of 10 cases?

       ii. Most likely cost (often coincides with the initial cost baseline).

      iii. Pessimistic scenario – what will be the highest cost in one of 10 cases?

    c. Model the dependencies between drivers, if desired. Current tools support multivariate distributions.

2. Event uncertainty:

    a. Walk through the project scenario and identify internal and external uncertainty factors that could impact project progress and costs, that is, factors not included in the cost baseline. Group factors into uncertainty domains (main drivers).

    b. For each driver, provide three-point estimates analogously to items i to iii above.

    c. Model the dependencies between drivers, if desired.

3. Generate a distribution from the three-point estimates items A and B. Current tools generate a range of distributions, including normal, log-normal, beta, and triangular ones.

4. Feed the distributions into the tools for Monte Carlo simulation. The Monte Carlo simulation generates a cumulative probability distribution of the total simulated project cost.

5. From the cumulative probability distribution, read off the desired pX values for cost. These values are used for decisions on uncertainty reserves at different management levels. In large public sector projects, the p50 cost is often given by the sponsor (e.g. the Department of Finance) to the project owner (e.g. a public service organization) as the budget limit. To be prepared for possible overruns of this limit, the sponsor will want to set a bad-case scenario limit, say, at p85. Sometimes, the project owner will impose a p35 estimate as the target for the project manager, the point being that the project should be managed on a day-to-day basis relative to a target that does not incorporate any uncertainty reserves.

References

1. M. Jørgensen, "A review of studies on expert estimation of software development effort," *J. Systems and Software*, vol. 70, no. 1–2, pp. 37–60, 2004.
2. M. Jørgensen, "Practical guidelines for expert-judgment-based software effort estimation," *IEEE Software*, vol. 22, no. 3, pp. 57–63, 2005.
3. D. Kahneman and A. Tversky, "Subjective probability: A judgment of representativeness," *Cognitive Psychology*, vol. 3, no. 3, 1972.
4. K. Kirtopoulos, V. Leopoulos, and V. Diamantas, "PERT vs. Monte Carlo simulation along with the suitable distribution effect," *Interntional J. Project Organisation and Management*, vol. 1, no. 1, pp. 24–46, 2008.
5. S. McConnell, *Software Estimation: Demystifying the Black Art.* Microsoft Press, 2006.
6. K.H. Teigen, M. Juanchich, and A.H. Riege, "Improbable outcomes: Infrequent or extraordinary?" *Cognition*, vol. 127, no. 1, 2013.

Chapter 7
Benefit and Cost Periodized: Stretching Your Points

Planning is bringing the future into the present, so that you can do
something about it *now*.

ALAN LAKEIN

Abstract When you estimate the life cycle cost and benefit of your software product, your stakeholders should not only be assured *that* you will deliver value, but also be informed *when* that value is expected to manifest itself. Periodization is a common method for showing when a return of investment is expected, and one is often careful to express the present value of future cash (net present value) in such deliberations. This chapter shows how to carry out periodization using points. Periodized points then amount to plan templates that can be instantiated with monetary values according to most likely, bad-case, and good-case uncertainty assessments.

7.1 Introduction

In all our discussions so far, we considered cost and benefit timeless quantities. However, cost will be spent and benefit will be earned not in one go, but over time. Further, the rate of earning and expenditures will most likely vary over time, and during development there will be mostly expenditures and little earning. To understand and control the project's influence on business investments and earnings, it is important to sequence out both cost estimates and benefit estimates in time. This procedure is called *periodization*. We will periodize our points-based estimates.

The time frame of the benefit and cost estimates we have been considering up until now needs to be clarified: since both cost and benefit estimates now include the post-deployment period, which can have longer and more variable time spans than development, we must be explicit about the period for which we are providing estimates.

The time frame is often explicit in the business case, say, if the business case is founded in a strategic period (see the agile fractal in Fig. 2.6 again). For example, the business case could specify that the system developed by the project should yield its estimated returns by the end of four years from the project start. If that is the case, one should consider how the estimates are distributed in time in the given time frame.

© The Author(s) 2021
J. E. Hannay, *Benefit/Cost-Driven Agile Software Development*,
Simula SpringerBriefs on Computing 8,
https://doi.org/10.1007/978-3-030-74218-8_7

7.2 Periodization

It is common to assess the progress of a project at regular intervals, and finance departments will be interested in annual, biannual, tertiary, or quarterly updates. Since we are agile and plan to release functionality quite often, let us assume that we would like to plan and assess the project at quarterly intervals. Our four-year example therefore covers 16 periods, and we illustrate by periodizing our estimates in Fig. 3.16 (p. 39) into these 16 periods.

Rather than redoing all the estimates in the 16-fold, we suggest using the existing estimates and distributing them over the 16 periods. For this, one can use predefined periodization profiles. Figure 7.1 illustrates periodization profiles for benefit. For example, the functionality of a new information technology system usually takes time to learn, and skill acquisition in such tasks can plateau after a while, as expressed in the profile 'delay with plateau'. Other tasks can inspire quick learning with or without an ensuing lack of enthusiasm for performing the task ('beginners' enthusiasm and deterioration' and 'immediate effect with linear increase and plateau'). If there is little insight into how benefit will be distributed in time, one can use a uniform profile. The general shapes of the benefit realization profiles in Fig. 7.1 are inspired by learning and skill building theories [4]. However, so far, there is a lack of empirical evidence to validate the profiles, so they must be treated as suggestions to be adapted according to any insights the stakeholders could have.

For cost, one can use profiles such as those exemplified in Fig. 7.2. In these examples, we assume that construction finishes within one period, since periods coincide with releases, but one can adapt one's own cost periodization for development as desired. For example, the 'High development (1 period) with low decreasing post-deployment' profile expresses the expectation that development will be intense and that post-deployment costs will be much lower and decrease over time, while 'Low development (1 period) with increasing post deployment' expresses the expectation that a short-resourced development period results in greater post-deployment costs. If one has no inkling about how cost will be distributed over periods, one can use the 'one-period development with uniform post deployment' profile.

7.2.1 Periodization of Points

Let us assume that the estimates for our running example were given for a four-year time frame, and that it will take 16 periods for the total amount of an epic's points to be spent or realized. You can see some of the profiles applied to the size points (SP) and benefit points (BP) of epic *E3* in the upper panel in Fig. 7.3. The size points are distributed using the 'High development (1 period) with low decreasing post deployment' profile. The benefit points towards objective *Obj1* are distributed using the 'Beginner's enthusiasm and deterioration' profile, benefit points towards *Obj2* are distributed using the 'Uniform with delay' profile, and benefit points towards *Obj3* are distributed using 'Immediate effect with linear increase and plateau'.

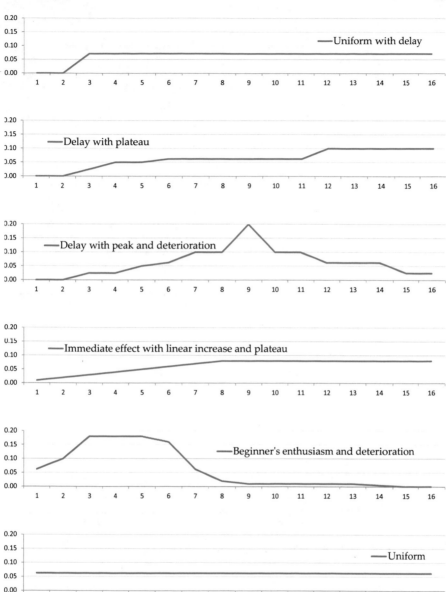

Fig. 7.1 Benefit realization profiles.

The 'Sum' column is the total amount of *E3*'s points periodized in the 16 periods (four years). Since the construction in this example is planned for one period, benefit starts being realized one period after development starts, leaving one period less for realization and leading to a sum less than the maximum possible for 16 periods (rightmost column, which corresponds to the points for *E3* in Figure 3.16). This

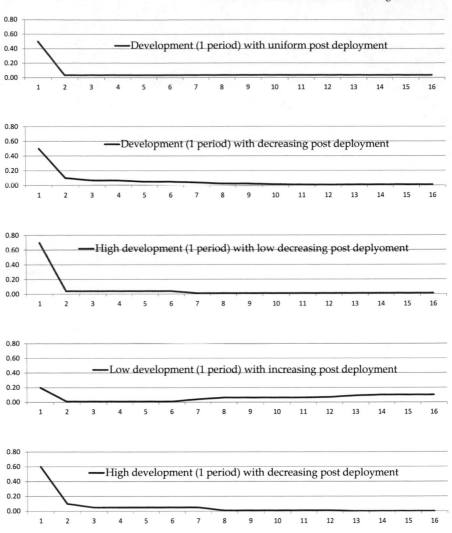

Fig. 7.2 Cost periodization profiles.

result does not mean that the project will not deliver the total estimated benefit – only that it will not do so within four years, which happens to be the time frame the sponsor has imposed on the project, say, for control purposes. So, unless the system is shut down, both cost and benefit will continue to develop beyond the time frame of four years, or 16 periods.

We ignore the blue numbers for now.

discount factor: 1		1	2	3	4	5	6	7	8	9	10	11	12	13	14	15	16	sum	max
E3																			
discounted SP		2.10	0.12	0.12	0.12	0.12	0.12	0.03	0.03	0.03	0.03	0.03	0.03	0.03	0.03	0.03	0.03	3.00	3.00
discounted BP	Obj1		0.93	1.48	2.67	2.67	2.67	2.37	0.93	0.30	0.15	0.15	0.15	0.15	0.15	0.07	0.00	14.83	14.83
	Obj2		0.02	0.05	0.07	0.09	0.11	0.14	0.16	0.18	0.18	0.18	0.18	0.18	0.18	0.18	0.18	2.11	2.30
	Obj3		0.00	0.00	0.44	0.44	0.44	0.44	0.44	0.44	0.44	0.44	0.44	0.44	0.44	0.44	0.44	5.73	6.18
net discounted points		-2.10	0.83	1.41	3.06	3.08	3.10	2.92	1.50	0.89	0.74	0.74	0.74	0.74	0.74	0.67	0.59	19.67	20.30

discount factor: 1.025		1	2	3	4	5	6	7	8	9	10	11	12	13	14	15	16	sum	max
E3																			
discounted SP		2.05	0.11	0.11	0.11	0.11	0.10	0.03	0.02	0.02	0.02	0.02	0.02	0.02	0.02	0.02	0.02	2.82	2.02
discounted BP	Obj1		0.88	1.38	2.42	2.36	2.30	2.00	0.76	0.24	0.12	0.11	0.11	0.11	0.10	0.05	0.00	12.93	14.83
	Obj2		0.02	0.04	0.06	0.08	0.10	0.12	0.13	0.15	0.14	0.14	0.14	0.13	0.13	0.13	0.12	1.64	2.30
	Obj3		0.00	0.00	0.40	0.39	0.38	0.37	0.36	0.35	0.34	0.34	0.33	0.32	0.31	0.30	0.30	4.50	6.18
net discounted points		-2.05	0.79	1.31	2.77	2.72	2.68	2.46	1.23	0.71	0.58	0.57	0.55	0.54	0.53	0.46	0.40	16.25	21.28

Fig. 7.3 Periodization of the size points (SP) and benefit points (BP) for Epic *E3* – discount factor 1, that is, not discounted (top), discount factor 1.025 (bottom).

7.2.2 Present Value of Future Cash

When investing cash, one should take into account the fact that future cash is not worth as much as present cash, because cash received in the future cannot be invested as present cash can. Indeed, present value considerations highlight the importance of incremental development over big bang delivery [1]. The second table in Fig. 7.3 shows the same periodization of *E3*, but takes into account the present value of future cash. Each period depreciates cash by 0.25%, assuming the potential for investing present cash at 1% per annum.[1]

7.2.3 Points Templates

Figure 7.4 presents a points template in a spreadsheet that can be instantiated with monetary values for benefit points and size points. The blue bottom row presents the computed values of the net points for each period, that is, the benefit points minus the size points. These blue figures have no meaning until one instantiates the benefit points and size points with monetary values. When instantiated, those figures will compute the net discounted cash. The point of these templates is that one can instantiate them with different monetary values to reflect different scenarios.

---

[1] This example follows the deprecation rate used in the example of [1]. Real rates will often be higher and can be set accordingly.

92   7 Benefit and Cost Periodized: Stretching Your Points

discount factor: 1.025	1	2	3	4	5	6	7	8	9	10	11	12	13	14	15	16	sum
E3																	
discounted SP	2.05	0.11	0.11	0.11	0.11	0.10	0.03	0.02	0.02	0.02	0.02	0.02	0.02	0.02	0.02	0.02	**2.82**
discounted BP Obj1		0.88	1.38	2.42	2.36	2.30	2.00	0.76	0.24	0.12	0.11	0.11	0.11	0.10	0.05	0.00	**12.93**
Obj2		0.02	0.04	0.06	0.08	0.10	0.12	0.13	0.15	0.14	0.14	0.14	0.13	0.13	0.13	0.12	**1.64**
Obj3		0.00	0.00	0.40	0.39	0.38	0.37	0.36	0.35	0.34	0.34	0.33	0.32	0.31	0.30	0.30	**4.50**
net discounted points	-2.05	0.79	1.31	2.77	2.72	2.68	2.46	1.23	0.71	0.58	0.57	0.55	0.54	0.53	0.46	0.40	**16.25**
E7																	
discounted SP	2.93	0.48	0.23	0.23	0.22	0.22	0.21	0.04	0.04	0.04	0.04	0.04	0.00	0.00	0.00	0.00	**4.70**
discounted BP Obj1		0.00	0.00	0.59	0.58	0.57	0.55	0.54	0.52	0.51	0.50	0.49	0.48	0.46	0.45	0.44	**6.69**
Obj2		0.00	0.00	0.21	0.20	0.40	0.48	0.75	0.74	1.44	0.70	0.68	0.42	0.41	0.40	0.15	**6.98**
Obj3		0.00	0.00	0.22	0.44	0.43	0.52	0.51	0.49	0.48	0.47	0.46	0.72	0.70	0.68	0.67	**6.78**
net discounted points	-2.93	-0.48	-0.23	0.80	1.00	1.17	1.34	1.76	1.72	2.39	1.63	1.59	1.61	1.57	1.53	1.26	**15.74**
E2																	
discounted SP	5.46	0.30	0.30	0.29	0.28	0.28	0.07	0.07	0.06	0.06	0.06	0.06	0.06	0.06	0.06	0.05	**7.52**
discounted BP Obj1		0.88	1.38	2.42	2.36	2.30	2.00	0.76	0.24	0.12	0.11	0.11	0.11	0.10	0.05	0.00	**12.93**
Obj2		1.44	2.24	3.94	3.84	3.75	3.25	1.24	0.39	0.19	0.18	0.18	0.18	0.17	0.08	0.00	**21.05**
Obj3		0.37	0.57	1.01	0.98	0.96	0.83	0.32	0.10	0.05	0.05	0.05	0.04	0.04	0.02	0.00	**5.39**
net discounted points	-5.46	2.38	3.89	7.07	6.90	6.73	6.01	2.25	0.66	0.29	0.28	0.28	0.27	0.26	0.10	-0.05	**31.85**
net Release 1:	-10.44																
E4																	
discounted SP		2.38	0.46	0.30	0.29	0.22	0.21	0.16	0.10	0.10	0.06	0.04	0.04	0.04	0.03	0.03	**4.46**
discounted BP Obj1			0.05	0.10	0.15	0.19	0.24	0.28	0.32	0.35	0.34	0.34	0.33	0.32	0.31	0.30	**3.63**
Obj2			0.09	0.17	0.24	0.32	0.39	0.45	0.52	0.57	0.56	0.55	0.53	0.52	0.51	0.50	**5.91**
Obj3			0.02	0.04	0.07	0.09	0.10	0.12	0.14	0.15	0.15	0.15	0.14	0.14	0.14	0.13	**1.59**
net discounted points		-2.38	-0.30	0.01	0.16	0.38	0.52	0.69	0.87	0.98	1.00	0.99	0.97	0.94	0.92	0.90	**6.66**
E8																	
discounted SP		5.33	0.30	0.29	0.28	0.28	0.27	0.07	0.06	0.06	0.06	0.06	0.06	0.06	0.06	0.05	**7.28**
discounted BP Obj1			0.08	0.13	0.22	0.22	0.21	0.19	0.07	0.02	0.01	0.01	0.01	0.01	0.01	0.00	**1.20**
Obj2			0.53	0.83	1.46	1.43	1.39	1.21	0.46	0.14	0.07	0.07	0.07	0.07	0.06	0.03	**7.82**
Obj3			0.00	0.00	0.35	0.35	0.68	0.82	1.29	1.25	2.45	1.19	1.16	0.71	0.69	0.68	**11.62**
net discounted points		-5.33	0.32	0.67	1.76	1.72	2.01	2.15	1.75	1.36	2.47	1.21	1.18	0.73	0.71	0.66	**13.37**
E1																	
discounted SP		4.57	0.74	0.36	0.35	0.34	0.34	0.33	0.06	0.06	0.06	0.06	0.06	0.00	0.00	0.00	**7.34**
discounted BP Obj1			0.00	0.00	0.20	0.40	0.39	0.47	0.46	0.45	0.44	0.43	0.42	0.65	0.63	0.62	**5.54**
Obj2			0.33	0.52	0.91	0.89	0.87	0.75	0.29	0.09	0.04	0.04	0.04	0.04	0.04	0.02	**4.89**
Obj3			0.00	0.00	0.22	0.21	0.42	0.51	0.79	0.77	1.51	0.73	0.72	0.44	0.43	0.42	**7.15**
net discounted points		-4.57	-0.41	0.16	0.98	1.16	1.34	1.40	1.47	1.25	1.93	1.14	1.12	1.13	1.10	1.05	**10.24**
net Release 2: -12.28																	
E5																	
discounted SP		8.45	0.47	0.46	0.45	0.44	0.43	0.10	0.10	0.10	0.10	0.09	0.09	0.09	0.09		**11.46**
discounted BP Obj1			0.00	0.00	0.04	0.04	0.04	0.04	0.04	0.04	0.04	0.04	0.04	0.04	0.03	0.03	**0.42**
Obj2			0.20	0.30	0.54	0.52	0.51	0.44	0.17	0.05	0.03	0.03	0.02	0.02	0.02		**2.85**
Obj3			0.23	0.46	0.67	0.87	1.06	1.25	1.42	1.58	1.54	1.51	1.47	1.43	1.40		**14.89**
net discounted points		-8.45	-0.04	0.30	0.80	1.00	1.19	1.62	1.52	1.57	1.51	1.47	1.44	1.40	1.37		**6.71**
E6																	
discounted SP		2.41	0.12	0.11	0.11	0.11	0.11	0.42	0.63	0.62	0.60	0.59	0.64	0.81	0.88		**8.17**
discounted BP Obj1			0.00	0.00	0.08	0.15	0.14	0.18	0.17	0.17	0.16	0.16	0.16	0.24	0.24		**1.85**
Obj2			0.00	0.00	0.12	0.12	0.24	0.29	0.45	0.44	0.85	0.42	0.41	0.25	0.24		**3.82**
Obj3			0.00	0.00	0.38	0.37	0.36	0.35	0.34	0.34	0.33	0.32	0.31	0.30	0.30		**3.71**
net discounted points		-2.41	-0.12	-0.11	0.47	0.53	0.64	0.40	0.33	0.32	0.74	0.31	0.23	-0.01	-0.10		**1.21**
net Release 3: -10.86																	
total discounted SP	10.44	13.17	13.01	2.17	2.12	1.99	1.67	1.22	0.88	1.08	1.02	0.98	0.92	0.91	1.06	1.12	**53.75**
total discounted BP	0.00	3.59	6.72	13.49	15.83	17.09	16.87	12.53	10.09	9.70	10.79	9.00	8.38	7.73	7.28	6.61	**155.79**
total disc. SP-BP	-10.44	-9.58	-6.29	11.32	13.71	15.10	15.21	11.30	9.21	8.71	9.77	8.02	7.47	6.83	6.22	5.49	**102.04**

Fig. 7.4 Points template for backlog at project initiation, with the ordered initial release plan with size points (SP) and benefit points (BP) periodized over 16 periods (four periods per year). Net present value is discounted at 0.25% per period (1% per year). The blue figures have no meaning until one instantiates the points and size points with monetary values.

Epic	Benefit	Cost	Benefit/Cost
E3	7.23	2.35	3.08
E7	8.77	3.91	2.24
E2	14.01	6.25	2.24
E4	5.37	3.91	1.37
E8	8.28	6.25	1.32
E1	7.70	6.25	1.23
E5	9.34	10.16	0.92
E6	4.80	10.16	0.47
Total	65.50	49.25	1.33

Fig. 7.5 Benefit/cost in terms of money at p50, where 1 benefit point = 0.31 million and 1 size point = 0.78 million.

7.3 Periodizing Planned Returns

In the project initiation phase, the sponsor and project owner need to plan when money should be invested and when they can expect a return. In other words, the budget needs to be expressed along a timeline. This is easily accomplished, using our benefit points and size points.

Assume that deployment has been planned in three increments, with the intention of maximizing benefit over cost early, as follows: Release 1, *E3*, *E7*, and *E2*; Release 2, *E4*, *E8*, and *E1*; and Release 3, *E5* and *E6*.

The sponsor would like a plan that is periodized in quarterly intervals and needs to see this plan from a four-year perspective for financial reasons. The cost and benefit profiles are applied based on the stakeholders' knowledge and experience.

Assume, further, that development takes one period. Figure 7.4 shows the size point and benefit point estimates for the eight epics of our example, periodized over 16 periods, according to the three releases, with 0.25% depreciation per period. The table is a point template, and the blue numbers are the resulting calculations of benefit points minus size points that have meaning once the points are instantiated with monetary values. We will instantiate them with monetary values in a moment.

Note how later releases leave less time for both spending and realizing benefit. However, with nonincremental development, one cannot deploy anything until after the fourth period, leaving even less time for realization. With nonincremental development, the sponsor generally will not be able to demand as short a time span for starting to evaluating a project's results and there will also be negligible project learning.

Since Fig. 7.4 is a template of points, one can instantiate it with various monetary values for size points and benefit points to view the initial plan form different perspectives. Let us see how this looks with p50 estimates for benefit points and size points, that is, 0.31 million per benefit point and 0.78 million per size point. Figure 7.5 presents our ordered epics with p50 monetary values.

Figure 7.6 shows the template in Fig. 7.4 instantiated with p50 monetary values. Figure 7.6 shows in detail what the project's initial estimates imply for each epic's earnings over time, and one can anticipate when the project as a whole will breaks even (between periods 12 and 13), according to the p50 estimates (the 'net discounted cash accumulated' row at the bottom and the blue curve). We can see what investments are needed (25.43 million over three periods) and the expected return on investment, which is net discounted cash divided by investments (6.34/25.43 = 0.25).

If one instantiates the 'total discounted SP' and 'total discounted BP' rows at the bottom of Fig. 7.4 with other monetary values generated from Monte Carlo simulations, one can compare expected outcomes at various levels of probability. Figure 7.7 (top) shows the periodized discounted cost estimates (in red) for the initial release plan according to p85 (0.84 million per size point), p50 (0.78 million per size point), and p35 (0.76 million per size point), as well as according to the initial estimate (0.6 million per size point) prior to uncertainty analysis. Regarding benefit, Fig. 7.7 (top panel) shows the periodized discounted benefit estimates according to p15 (0.29 million per benefit point), p50 (0.31 million per benefit point), and p65 (0.32 million per benefit point), as well as the initial benefit estimate (0.36 million per benefit point) prior to uncertainty analysis. By looking at how these curves move and where they intersect, one can predict expenditures and earnings and when the project breaks even according to various levels of certainty. For example, in a good-case scenario (benefit p65 and cost p35), breakeven occurs in period 11, while, in a bad-case scenario (benefit p15 and cost p85), the project does not quite break even within the 16 periods. Notice how the initial estimates without uncertainty analysis predict breaking even at around seven periods. In this example, these initial estimates are not likely if one takes into account the uncertainty assessments that underlie the Monte Carlo simulations in Chapter 6.

The project owner can now view the project's financial boundaries in time by observing how the 'total net discounted points' row (blue) in Fig. 7.4 varies when the 'total discounted SP' and 'total discounted BP' rows are instantiated. Figure 7.7 (bottom) shows the corresponding curves for the net discounted cash estimates according to p50 and the good-case (benefit p65 and cost p35) and bad-case (benefit p15 and cost p85) estimates. The project owner can plan finances according to these boundaries and ask that project management aim for p50 or the good-case estimate and insist that notice be given and steps taken whenever the project strays from the boundaries.

7.4 Monitoring and Adjusting Planned Returns

When a project is underway, one can monitor its progress relative to its budget and boundaries of financial tolerance set up above. As an example, consider detailing the epics of Release 1 into stories, as we did in Chapter 5, summarized here in Fig. 7.8. It is evident that story *E7C* provides little benefit to cost and is wasteful, so we eliminate it from the backlog. For the vacated capacity in Release 1, we elaborate epic *E4* originally planned for Release 2 and find that stories *E4A* and *E4D* give the

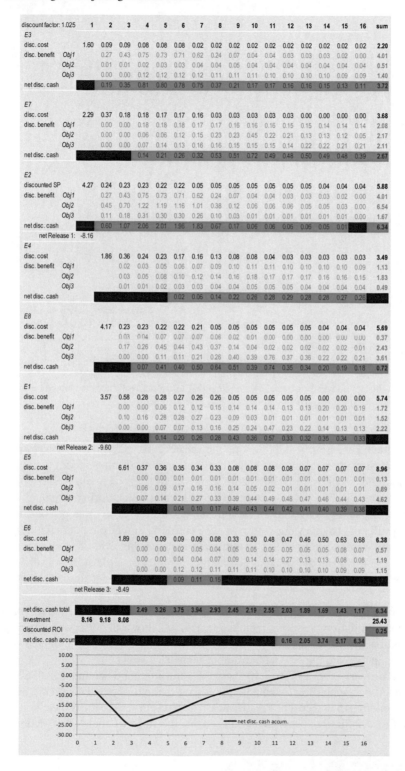

Fig. 7.6 Table 7.4 is instantiated with Monte Carlo p50 estimates of 0.31 million per benefit point and 0.78 million per size point.

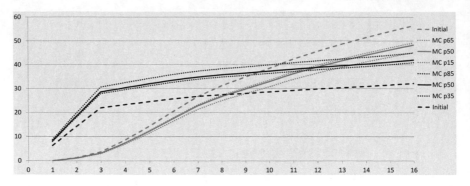

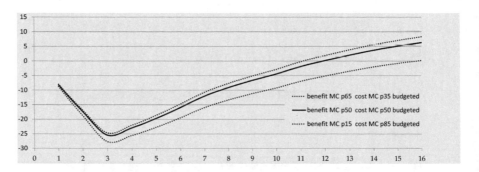

Fig. 7.7 Project budget and boundaries of financial tolerance, with net discounted cash over 16 periods and Monte Carlo p50 and good- and bad-case estimates.

best value for the money and fit within the vacated space. The remaining stories *E4B* and, *E4C* provide questionable benefit to cost, and we eliminate them too.

Epics *E6* and *E5* are questionable, as a whole (Figs. 7.5 and 7.8). Looking at the prognosis in Fig. 7.4, we find that *E6* generates value during three periods but nets out negatively. One could decommission *E6* after these three periods, but that would still not provide value over cost. The periodization also renders *E1* seemingly wasteful. We choose, however, to eliminate waste at the level of stories, not epics, because in this example we assume that there could be viable stories, even in epics that are low on benefit/cost overall. So, *E6*, *E5*, and *E1* are left in until elaboration time.

Just as the point template in Fig. 7.4 shows the discounted periodized backlog at project initiation, the point template in Fig. 7.9 shows the discounted periodized revised backlog at construction time for Release 1, with waste eliminated. Again, one can instantiate Fig. 7.9 with different monetary values.

The brown curves in Fig. 7.10 show the resulting net discounted cash estimates for Release 1, according to the p50, good-case (benefit p65 and cost p35), and bad-case (benefit p15 and cost p85) estimates. The bluc curves are the project boundaries from Fig. 7.7 (bottom panel). One can see that the steps we took when planning Re-

Epic	Story	Benefit	Part of Epic	Benefit	Cost	Part of Epic	Cost	Benefit/Cost	
E3		7.23			2.35		3.08		
	E3A		0.7	5.06		0.6	1.41	3.60	
	E3B		0.3	2.17		0.4	0.94	2.31	
E7		8.77			3.91		2.24		
	E7A		0.6	5.26		0.2	0.78	6.73	
	E7B		0.3	2.63		0.3	1.17	2.24	
	E7C		0.1	0.88		0.5	1.95	0.45	
E2		14.01			6.25		2.24		
	E2A		0.5	7.01		0.2	1.25	5.60	
	E2B		0.1	1.40		0.2	1.25	1.12	
	E2C		0.2	2.80		0.3	1.88	1.49	
	E2D		0.2	2.80		0.3	1.88	1.49	
E4		5.37			3.91		1.37		
E8		8.28			6.25		1.32		
E1		7.70			6.25		1.23		
E5		9.34			10.16		0.92		
E6		4.80			10.16		0.47		
Total		65.50		30.01	49.25		12.51	1.33	2.40
E4		5.37			3.91		1.37		
	E4A		0.3	1.61		0.2	0.78	2.06	
	E4B		0.2	1.07		0.3	1.17	0.92	
	E4C		0.3	1.61		0.4	1.56	1.03	
	E4D		0.2	1.07		0.1	0.39	2.75	

Fig. 7.8 Release 1 revised at p50, with 1 benefit point = 0.31 million and 1 size point = 0.78 million.

lease 1 are paying off relative to the project boundaries. For example, the brown projected p50 curve is above the blue planned good-case curve, and the breakeven point according to p50 is now around period 10, instead of around period 12. (The revised backlog has fewer size points and benefit points. The brown curves are based on recomputed Monte Carlo pX estimates on this revised backlog, which gives slightly different pX values from those for the full backlog.)

7.5 Adjusting Values According to Project Experience

A key point of agile is project learning, which pertains to a range of management aspects, both motivational and social, to get a feel for how to best run the complex system that a project is, as well as aspects of development and stakeholder experience. For our discussion, we are interested in how to express project experience in adjusting the monetary value of benefit points and size points.

After Release 1 is completed, you will have the actual values for the amount a size point costs in that release. You should use that information when refining and

discount factor: 1.025 1.025	1	2	3	4	5	6	7	8	9	10	11	12	13	14	15	16	sum
E3																	
discounted SP	2.05	0.11	0.11	0.11	0.11	0.10	0.03	0.02	0.02	0.02	0.02	0.02	0.02	0.02	0.02	0.02	**2.82**
discounted BP *Obj1*		0.88	1.38	2.42	2.36	2.30	2.00	0.76	0.24	0.12	0.11	0.11	0.11	0.10	0.05	0.00	12.93
Obj2		0.02	0.04	0.06	0.08	0.10	0.12	0.13	0.15	0.14	0.14	0.14	0.13	0.13	0.13	0.12	1.64
Obj3		0.00	0.00	0.40	0.39	0.38	0.37	0.36	0.35	0.34	0.34	0.33	0.32	0.31	0.30	0.30	4.50
net discounted points	-2.05	0.79	1.31	2.77	2.72	2.68	2.46	1.23	0.71	0.58	0.57	0.55	0.54	0.53	0.46	0.40	**16.25**
E7AB																	
discounted SP	1.46	0.24	0.12	0.11	0.11	0.11	0.11	0.02	0.02	0.02	0.02	0.02	0.00	0.00	0.00	0.00	**2.35**
discounted BP *Obj1*		0.00	0.00	0.53	0.52	0.51	0.50	0.48	0.47	0.46	0.45	0.44	0.43	0.42	0.41	0.40	6.02
Obj2		0.00	0.00	0.19	0.18	0.36	0.44	0.68	0.66	1.29	0.63	0.62	0.38	0.37	0.36	0.14	6.28
Obj3		0.00	0.00	0.20	0.39	0.38	0.47	0.46	0.45	0.43	0.42	0.41	0.65	0.63	0.61	0.60	6.10
net discounted points	-1.46	-0.24	-0.12	0.81	0.99	1.14	1.29	1.60	1.56	2.17	1.48	1.45	1.45	1.41	1.38	1.14	**16.05**
E4AD																	
discounted SP	0.73	0.14	0.09	0.09	0.07	0.06	0.05	0.03	0.03	0.02	0.01	0.01	0.01	0.01	0.01	0.01	1.38
discounted BP *Obj1*		0.03	0.05	0.08	0.10	0.12	0.14	0.16	0.18	0.18	0.17	0.17	0.16	0.16	0.16	0.15	2.01
Obj2		0.04	0.09	0.12	0.16	0.20	0.23	0.26	0.29	0.29	0.28	0.27	0.27	0.26	0.25	0.25	3.28
Obj3		0.01	0.02	0.03	0.04	0.05	0.06	0.07	0.08	0.08	0.08	0.07	0.07	0.07	0.07	0.07	0.88
net discounted points	-0.73	-0.06	0.07	0.14	0.24	0.31	0.39	0.47	0.52	0.52	0.52	0.50	0.49	0.48	0.47	0.46	4.78
E2																	
discounted SP	5.46	0.30	0.30	0.29	0.28	0.28	0.07	0.07	0.06	0.06	0.06	0.06	0.06	0.06	0.06	0.05	**7.52**
discounted BP *Obj1*		0.88	1.38	2.42	2.36	2.30	2.00	0.76	0.24	0.12	0.11	0.11	0.11	0.10	0.05	0.00	12.93
Obj2		1.44	2.24	3.94	3.84	3.75	3.25	1.24	0.39	0.19	0.18	0.18	0.17	0.08	0.00		21.05
Obj3		0.37	0.57	1.01	0.98	0.96	0.83	0.32	0.10	0.05	0.05	0.05	0.04	0.04	0.02	0.00	5.39
net discounted points	-5.46	2.38	3.89	7.07	6.90	6.73	6.01	2.25	0.66	0.29	0.28	0.28	0.27	0.26	0.10	-0.05	**31.85**
net Release 1:	-9.71																
E8																	
discounted SP		5.33	0.30	0.29	0.28	0.28	0.27	0.07	0.06	0.06	0.06	0.06	0.06	0.06	0.06	0.05	**7.28**
discounted BP *Obj1*			0.08	0.13	0.22	0.22	0.21	0.19	0.07	0.02	0.01	0.01	0.01	0.01	0.01	0.00	1.20
Obj2			0.53	0.83	1.46	1.43	1.39	1.21	0.46	0.14	0.07	0.07	0.07	0.07	0.06	0.03	7.82
Obj3			0.00	0.00	0.35	0.35	0.68	0.82	1.29	1.25	2.45	1.19	1.16	0.71	0.69	0.68	11.62
net discounted points		-5.33	0.32	0.67	1.76	1.72	2.01	2.15	1.75	1.36	2.47	1.21	1.18	0.73	0.71	0.66	**13.37**
E1																	
discounted SP		4.57	0.74	0.36	0.35	0.34	0.34	0.33	0.06	0.06	0.06	0.06	0.06	0.00	0.00	0.00	**7.34**
discounted BP *Obj1*			0.00	0.00	0.20	0.40	0.39	0.47	0.46	0.45	0.44	0.43	0.42	0.65	0.63	0.62	5.54
Obj2			0.33	0.52	0.91	0.89	0.87	0.75	0.29	0.09	0.04	0.04	0.04	0.04	0.04	0.02	4.89
Obj3			0.00	0.00	0.22	0.21	0.42	0.51	0.79	0.77	1.51	0.73	0.72	0.44	0.43	0.42	7.15
net discounted points		-4.57	-0.41	0.16	0.98	1.16	1.34	1.40	1.47	1.25	1.93	1.14	1.12	1.13	1.10	1.05	**10.24**
net Release 2:	-9.90																
E5																	
discounted SP			8.45	0.47	0.46	0.45	0.44	0.43	0.10	0.10	0.10	0.10	0.09	0.09	0.09	0.09	**11.46**
discounted BP *Obj1*				0.00	0.00	0.04	0.04	0.04	0.04	0.04	0.04	0.04	0.04	0.04	0.03	0.03	0.42
Obj2				0.20	0.30	0.54	0.52	0.51	0.44	0.17	0.05	0.03	0.03	0.03	0.02	0.02	2.85
Obj3				0.23	0.46	0.67	0.87	1.06	1.25	1.42	1.58	1.54	1.51	1.47	1.43	1.40	14.89
net discounted points			-8.45	-0.04	0.30	0.80	1.00	1.19	1.62	1.52	1.57	1.51	1.47	1.44	1.40	1.37	**6.71**
E6																	
discounted SP			2.41	0.12	0.11	0.11	0.11	0.11	0.42	0.63	0.62	0.60	0.59	0.64	0.81	0.88	**8.17**
discounted BP *Obj1*				0.00	0.00	0.08	0.15	0.14	0.18	0.17	0.17	0.16	0.16	0.16	0.24	0.24	1.85
Obj2				0.00	0.00	0.12	0.12	0.24	0.29	0.45	0.44	0.85	0.42	0.41	0.25	0.24	3.82
Obj3				0.00	0.00	0.38	0.37	0.36	0.35	0.34	0.34	0.33	0.32	0.31	0.30	0.30	3.71
net discounted points			-2.41	-0.12	-0.11	0.47	0.53	0.64	0.40	0.33	0.32	0.74	0.31	0.23	-0.01	-0.10	**1.21**
net Release 3:	-10.86																
total discounted SP	9.71	10.70	12.52	1.84	1.78	1.73	1.40	1.07	0.79	0.98	0.95	0.93	0.89	0.88	1.04	1.10	**48.32**
total discounted BP	0.00	3.67	6.72	13.31	15.55	16.73	16.42	11.99	9.49	9.01	10.09	8.32	7.72	7.09	6.65	6.02	**148.79**
total disc. SP-BP	-9.71	-7.03	-5.80	11.47	13.78	15.00	15.02	10.92	8.71	8.02	9.14	7.39	6.83	6.20	5.61	4.92	**100.47**

Fig. 7.9 Points template for backlog at the start of Release 1 ordered into the release plan, with size points (SP) and benefit points (BP) periodized over 16 periods (four periods per year). Net present value is discounted at 0.25% per period (1% per year). The blue figures have no meaning until one instantiates the benefit points and size points with monetary values.

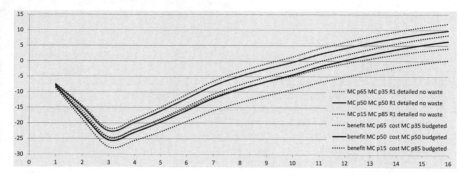

Fig. 7.10 Projected net discounted cash at the start of Release 1 with waste (*E7C*, *E4B*, and *E4C*) eliminated (brown) for the good case (p65 0.33 per BP, p35 0.76 per SP), the expected case (p50 0.32 per BP, 0.79 per SP), and the bad case (p15 0.30 per BP, cost p85 0.84 per SP). The project budget and boundaries of financial tolerance are in blue.

adjusting the backlog for Release 2. You can instantiate size points with the actual cost directly, or you can use the actual cost as the basis for a new Monte Carlo simulation to obtain adjusted pX estimates. If you want to be more advanced, you can use Bayesian statistics to integrate your present information (actual cost) with your past beliefs (previous estimated monetary value for size points).

By the time you have completed Release 2, stakeholders could have had time to gain experience with that part of the system deployed after Release 1. They could have opinions regarding both benefit and post-deployment costs, which you should incorporate into the monetary values with which you instantiate your point model.

As your project gains more experience, you can update your monetary values for the benefit points and size points, and, perhaps, uncertainty will decrease, that is, some of your three-point estimates can be narrowed [3]. When running fresh Monte Carlo simulations, you can monitor your project according to fresh information to the best of the project's knowledge at any point of time.

7.6 Optimizing the Backlog for Periodization

In our running example, we ordered the backlog according to the basic benefit-cost ratio, but, in reality, periodization impacts the optimal sequence of construction. This book integrates our points-based approach with Denne and Cleland-Huang's *Incremental Funding Method* [2, 1], which you can consult to find out how to order your points-based backlog even better in light of periodization.

References

1. M. Denne and J. Cleland-Huang, *Software by Numbers: Low-Risk, High-Return Development.* Prentice Hall, 2003.
2. M. Denne and J. Cleland-Huang, "The incremental funding method: Data-driven software development," *IEEE Software*, vol. 21, no. 3, pp. 39–47, May/June 2004.
3. H. Erdogmus, "The economic impact of learning and flexibility on process decisions," *IEEE Software*, vol. 22, no. 6, pp. 76–83, November/December 2005.
4. K.A. Ericsson, "An introduction to Cambridge Handbook of Expertise and Expert Performance: Its development, organization, and content," in *The Cambridge Handbook of Expertise and Expert Performance*, K.A. Ericsson, N. Charness, P.J. Feltovich, and R.R. Hoffman, Eds.   Cambridge Univ. Press, 2006, ch. 1, pp. 3–20.

Chapter 8
Final Remarks

Benefit points complement the concept of points-based estimation. We showed how to use points estimates for both benefit and cost in various project and portfolio management activities. One can also adapt a range of other models that we did not cover (see e.g. [3, 1, 2]) to points-based estimates. Points-based estimates give rise to project management templates into which you can instantiate various monetary values, for example, various scenarios according to uncertainty assessments.

Benefit points make benefit estimation explicit. The strength of this approach over others is that benefit points provide an explicit link from the strategic level through the business case and down and into a project's product elements and backlogs.

In portfolio and project management there are opposing views. For example, the *earned business value management* regime provides a dashboard with indicators of project progress in terms of your estimates, regardless of exactly when and in what direction cash flows. It gives you metrics for the amount of estimated business value and functionality you are producing. The periodized regime, in contrast, provides a dashboard with indicators of when investment is needed and when a return is expected. These two dashboards represent opposing interests belonging to those who favour product, on the one hand, versus those who favour return, on the other hand. Differences in opinion regarding these views have likely resulted in many conflicts and can ultimately run projects aground. The good news is that you can now construct these dashboards using the same points-based data, data that all stakeholders of the project have produced and own jointly. This at least means that decisions can be made that are closer to what amounts to a common vision of product and process.

The lack of documented use of techniques that support benefits management and, in fact, the unfortunate dearth of benefits management at all imply that this book is a call for action. Since benefits management, at least in some form, is making its way into corporate and public service regulations, it is time to move beyond mere talk. Benefits management must manifest itself in concrete benefits management tasks whose effects can be monitored over time. The techniques in this book were designed to support benefits management in that way, but the important thing is that you do use benefits management techniques; if not those presented in this book,

© The Author(s) 2021   101
J. E. Hannay, *Benefit/Cost-Driven Agile Software Development*,
Simula SpringerBriefs on Computing 8,
https://doi.org/10.1007/978-3-030-74218-8_8

then perhaps other techniques or ones tailored to your organization that you develop
yourself.

References

1. S. Biffl, A. Aurum, B. Boehm, H. Erdogmus, and P. Grünbacher, Eds., *Value-Based Software Engineering.* Springer, 2006.
2. B. Boehm and L.G. Huang, "Value-based software engineering: A case study," *Computer*, vol. 36, no. 3, pp. 33–41, March 2003.
3. K.E. Wiegers, "First things first: Prioritizing requirements," *Software Development Magazine*, vol. 7, no. 9, pp. 24–30, September 1999.

Printed in the United States
by Baker & Taylor Publisher Services